Afghanistan

Other Books of Related Interest:

At Issue Series

Is Iran a Threat to Global Security?

Is There a New Cold War?

What Motivates Suicide Bombers?

Current Controversies Series

Afghanistan

Global Viewpoints

Drugs

The War in Iraq

Introducing Issues with Opposing Viewpoints Series

Afghanistan

Iran

National Security

War

Opposing Viewpoints Series

Islam

Pakistan

"Congress shall make no law ... abridging the freedom of speech, or of the press."

First Amendment to the U.S. Constitution

The basic foundation of our democracy is the First Amendment guarantee of freedom of expression. The Opposing Viewpoints Series is dedicated to the concept of this basic freedom and the idea that it is more important to practice it than to enshrine it.

Afghanistan

Noah Berlatsky, Book Editor

GREENHAVEN PRESS

A part of Gale, Cengage Learning

GALE
CENGAGE Learning™

Detroit • New York • San Francisco • New Haven, Conn • Waterville, Maine • London

958.101
AFG

Christine Nasso, *Publisher*
Elizabeth Des Chenes, *Managing Editor*

© 2011 Greenhaven Press, a part of Gale, Cengage Learning

Articles in Greenhaven Press anthologies are often edited for length to meet page requirements. In addition, original titles of these works are changed to clearly present the main thesis and to explicitly indicate the author's opinion. Every effort is made to ensure that Greenhaven Press accurately reflects the original intent of the authors. Every effort has been made to trace the owners of copyrighted material.

Cover image by AJ Wilhelm/National Geographic/Getty Images.

LIBRARY OF CONGRESS CATALOGING-IN-PUBLICATION DATA

Afghanistan / Noah Berlatsky, book editor.
    p. cm. -- (Opposing viewpoints)
    Includes bibliographical references and index.
    ISBN 978-0-7377-5102-4 (hardcover) -- ISBN 978-0-7377-5103-1 (pbk.)
    1. Afghanistan--Politics and government--2001- 2. Afghan War, 2001- I. Berlatsky, Noah.
    JQ1769.A15A325 2010
    958.104'7--dc22
                                                        2010016972

Printed in the United States of America
1 2 3 4 5 6 7 14 13 12 11 10

Contents

Chapter 1: What Is the Military Situation in Afghanistan?

Chapter 2: What Is the Status of Human Rights in Afghanistan?

Chapter 3: What Progress Is Afghanistan Making Toward Democracy?

Why Consider Opposing Viewpoints?

> "The only way in which a human being can make some approach to knowing the whole of a subject is by hearing what can be said about it by persons of every variety of opinion and studying all modes in which it can be looked at by every character of mind. No wise man ever acquired his wisdom in any mode but this."
>
> *John Stuart Mill*

In our media-intensive culture it is not difficult to find differing opinions. Thousands of newspapers and magazines and dozens of radio and television talk shows resound with differing points of view. The difficulty lies in deciding which opinion to agree with and which "experts" seem the most credible. The more inundated we become with differing opinions and claims, the more essential it is to hone critical reading and thinking skills to evaluate these ideas. Opposing Viewpoints books address this problem directly by presenting stimulating debates that can be used to enhance and teach these skills. The varied opinions contained in each book examine many different aspects of a single issue. While examining these conveniently edited opposing views, readers can develop critical thinking skills such as the ability to compare and contrast authors' credibility, facts, argumentation styles, use of persuasive techniques, and other stylistic tools. In short, the Opposing Viewpoints Series is an ideal way to attain the higher-level thinking and reading skills so essential in a culture of diverse and contradictory opinions.

In addition to providing a tool for critical thinking, Opposing Viewpoints books challenge readers to question their own strongly held opinions and assumptions. Most people form their opinions on the basis of upbringing, peer pressure, and personal, cultural, or professional bias. By reading carefully balanced opposing views, readers must directly confront new ideas as well as the opinions of those with whom they disagree. This is not to simplistically argue that everyone who reads opposing views will—or should—change his or her opinion. Instead, the series enhances readers' understanding of their own views by encouraging confrontation with opposing ideas. Careful examination of others' views can lead to the readers' understanding of the logical inconsistencies in their own opinions, perspective on why they hold an opinion, and the consideration of the possibility that their opinion requires further evaluation.

Evaluating Other Opinions

To ensure that this type of examination occurs, Opposing Viewpoints books present all types of opinions. Prominent spokespeople on different sides of each issue as well as well-known professionals from many disciplines challenge the reader. An additional goal of the series is to provide a forum for other, less known, or even unpopular viewpoints. The opinion of an ordinary person who has had to make the decision to cut off life support from a terminally ill relative, for example, may be just as valuable and provide just as much insight as a medical ethicist's professional opinion. The editors have two additional purposes in including these less known views. One, the editors encourage readers to respect others' opinions—even when not enhanced by professional credibility. It is only by reading or listening to and objectively evaluating others' ideas that one can determine whether they are worthy of consideration. Two, the inclusion of such viewpoints encourages the important critical thinking skill of objectively evaluating an author's credentials and bias. This evaluation will illuminate an author's reasons for taking a particular stance on an issue and will aid in readers' evaluation of the author's ideas.

It is our hope that these books will give readers a deeper understanding of the issues debated and an appreciation of the complexity of even seemingly simple issues when good and honest people disagree. This awareness is particularly important in a democratic society such as ours in which people enter into public debate to determine the common good. Those with whom one disagrees should not be regarded as enemies but rather as people whose views deserve careful examination and may shed light on one's own.

Thomas Jefferson once said that "difference of opinion leads to inquiry, and inquiry to truth." Jefferson, a broadly educated man, argued that "if a nation expects to be ignorant and free . . . it expects what never was and never will be." As individuals and as a nation, it is imperative that we consider the opinions of others and examine them with skill and discernment. The Opposing Viewpoints Series is intended to help readers achieve this goal.

David L. Bender and Bruno Leone,
Founders

Introduction

> "Al Qaeda was founded in 1988 by
> Osama bin Laden to consolidate the in-
> ternational network he established dur-
> ing the Afghan war. Its goals were the
> advancement of Islamic revolutions
> throughout the Muslim world and repel-
> ling foreign intervention in the Middle
> East."
>
> —Anti-Defamation League

The most recent phase of the United States' involvement with Afghanistan could be said to have begun on September 11, 2001, when terrorists flew hijacked passenger airliners into the World Trade Center and Pentagon buildings, killing thousands of Americans. The attacks were linked to al Qaeda, a radical Islamist terrorist network commanded by Saudi national Osama bin Laden. At the time of the September 11 attacks, Bin Laden was in Afghanistan, where the radical Islamist government, known as the Taliban, had given him safe haven. The United States invaded Afghanistan in early October 2001 in an effort to capture Bin Laden and crush al Qaeda and the Taliban.

Bin Laden's ties to Afghanistan began long before 2001, however. He first became involved in Afghan politics after the Soviet Union invaded Afghanistan in 1979. The Soviet invasion launched a nine-year war in which Muslims from around the Arab world came to fight on behalf of the Afghans against the atheist Soviet government. These Muslim soldiers became known as mujahideen, or "fighters for freedom." Bin Laden became a leader among them, operating a guesthouse in Pakistan that served as "a stopping-off point for Arab mujahideen fighters," according to a December 6, 2009, BBC News article. Eventually Bin Laden set up entire camps for mujahideen volunteers across the border in Afghanistan. These camps were called al Qaeda, which means "the base" in Arabic.

Because of its opposition to the Soviet Union—which was engaged in the Cold War with the United States—the United States supported the mujahideen, and especially after 1984 the Islamic fighters "began receiving substantial assistance in the form of weapons and training from the U.S. and other outside powers," according to a November 2008 article on the Web site of the U.S. Department of State. Bin Laden and the Afghan opposition certainly benefited in general from U.S. aid, and some have claimed that Bin Laden and al Qaeda were directly funded by the U.S. Central Intelligence Agency (CIA). In a July 8, 2005, article for the *Guardian*, Robin Cook stated, "Throughout the 80s [Bin Laden] was armed by the CIA and funded by the Saudis to wage jihad against the Russian occupation of Afghanistan." However, such a direct link is controversial. Steve Coll, author of *Ghost Wars: The Secret History of the CIA, Afghanistan, and Bin Laden, from the Soviet Invasion to September 10, 2001*, said "I did not discover any evidence of direct contact between CIA officers and Bin Laden during the 1980s," according to a quotation on the Web site 911myths . . . Reading Between the Lies (www.911myths.com).

Whether Bin Laden ever did or did not have a direct connection with the CIA, he was certainly a force in the Afghan resistance, participating in a number of battles and earning a reputation as a fierce fighter. The Soviet Union withdrew in defeat from Afghanistan in 1989. Bin Laden went back to Saudi Arabia, but "became disillusioned by the lack of recognition for his achievements," according to an article on the Biography Channel Web site. Bin Laden had long been strongly anti-Western, but throughout the 1990s, he became more and more radical, calling for violent attacks on America, Jews, and the Saudi royal family, and organizing a number of terror attacks. He was forced out of Saudi Arabia, and then out of the Republic of the Sudan.

Finally, in 1996, Bin Laden returned to Afghanistan, where the radical Islamist Taliban had recently taken control of the government. Operating from Afghanistan during the next several years, al Qaeda claimed to be involved in a number of deadly terrorist attacks, the most notable of which was a series of bombings at U.S. embassies in Africa in August 1998, resulting in hundreds of deaths. In response, President Bill Clinton ordered missile strikes in Afghanistan to kill Bin Laden. Bin Laden eluded the missiles by a few hours, however. Clinton several times contemplated another attack, but "chose not to act because of uncertainty that intelligence was good enough to find Bin Laden, and concern that a failed attack would only enhance his stature in the Arab world," according to John F. Harris, writing in the *Washington Post*.

Following the September 11 attacks and the U.S. invasion in October 2001, the Taliban government in Afghanistan was overthrown. Bin Laden himself was hunted down and forced to hole up in a mountainous region of Afghanistan known as Tora Bora. However, the United States failed to capture him, and he slipped across the border into Pakistan, where he continued to evade capture for years. In a report on November 30, 2009, the U.S. Senate Committee on Foreign Relations concluded that the United States had failed to commit enough troops to ensure Bin Laden's capture, and that "the failure to finish the job represents a lost opportunity that forever altered the course of the conflict in Afghanistan and the future of international terrorism, leaving the American people more vulnerable to terrorism, laying the foundation for today's protracted Afghan insurgency and inflaming the internal strife now endangering Pakistan."

As of the end of 2009, U.S. officials believed Bin Laden was still in Pakistan but could have been occasionally moving back across the border into Afghanistan, where a Taliban-led insurgency had risen up to fight against the U.S.-supported Afghan government. However, Bin Laden's precise where-abouts remained unknown. As Defense Secretary Robert Gates noted in a December 7, 2009, Associated Press report, "'If we did [know where he was], we'd go get him.'"

Bin Laden's association with Afghanistan highlights both the dangers and the importance of the country to the United States. The authors featured in *Opposing Viewpoints: Afghanistan* further address that nation's complexities in the following chapters: What Is the Military Situation in Afghanistan? What Is the Status of Human Rights in Afghanistan? What Progress Is Afghanistan Making Toward Democracy? and How Should the Drug Trade Be Confronted in Afghanistan? Answering these questions will clarify where Afghanistan has been in the past and what its future may hold.

VIEWPOINTS®
SERIES

CHAPTER 1

What Is the Military Situation in Afghanistan?

Chapter Preface

The U.S. invasion of Afghanistan in 2001 was eventually overshadowed by the U.S. invasion of Iraq in 2003. The United States continued to fight in Afghanistan, but Iraq—which for many years saw high levels of violence and teetered on the brink of full-scale civil war—received much more attention from media and government. In a January 30, 2008, report, the Center for American Progress referred to Afghanistan as "the forgotten front in the fight against global terrorism."

In his campaign for president, Barack Obama argued that American commitments in Iraq should be wound down and that Afghanistan should be moved to the center of American foreign policy priorities. In a campaign speech on July 15, 2008, Obama stated, "Now is the time for a responsible redeployment of our combat troops that pushes Iraq's leaders toward a political solution, rebuilds our military, and refocuses on Afghanistan and our broader security interests." Obama added, "Our troops and our NATO allies are performing heroically in Afghanistan, but I have argued for years that we lack the resources to finish the job because of our commitment to Iraq. That's what the chairman of the Joint Chiefs of Staff said earlier this month. And that's why, as president, I will make the fight against al Qaeda and the Taliban the top priority that it should be. This is a war that we have to win."

After being elected president in November 2008, Obama did in fact increase America's commitments in Afghanistan. In March 2009, he deployed four thousand additional troops to that nation in an effort to "bolster the Afghan army and turn up the heat on terrorists," according to an Associated Press report on March 27, 2009. Then, in December of that year, after a lengthy and much publicized policy review, Obama announced he would deploy an additional thirty thousand soldiers to Afghanistan. In explaining his decision in a speech at the U.S. Military Academy at West Point on December 1, 2009, Obama stated, "I make this decision because I am convinced that our security is at stake in Afghanistan and Pakistan. This is the epicenter of violent extremism practiced by al Qaeda. It is from here that we were attacked on 9/11, and it is from here that new attacks are being plotted as I speak. This is no idle danger; no hypothetical threat. In the last few months alone, we have apprehended extremists within our borders who were sent here from the border region of Afghanistan and Pakistan to commit new acts of terror. And this danger will only grow if the region slides backwards, and al Qaeda can operate with impunity. We must keep the pressure on al Qaeda, and to do that, we must increase the stability and capacity of our partners in the region."

At the same time that he committed more troops, Obama also set a timetable for withdrawal from Afghanistan. Gregor Peter Schmitz, writing in *Der Spiegel* on December 2, 2009, described Obama's plan as a "curious, double-pronged strategy. A rapid surge, set to be complete by next summer, coupled with a rapid draw-down, planned to already begin in 2011." Schmitz added that many critics wondered "how seriously will the enemy take the surge when the withdrawal date has already been set?"

Both Obama's decision to increase the U.S. presence in Afghanistan and his decision to set a definite withdrawal date have been controversial. The following viewpoints put these issues in context by discussing other strategic debates about U.S. involvement in Afghanistan.

| "*The situation is poised between a war difficult to win and an unlikely peace.*"

The Taliban Are Winning in Afghanistan

Antonio Giustozzi

Antonio Giustozzi is a researcher at the Crisis States Research Centre of the London School of Economics and Political Science and is the author of Koran, Kalashnikov and Laptop: The Neo-Taliban Insurgency in Afghanistan. *In the following viewpoint, he argues that the Taliban's success has been achieved not because of military proficiency or outside aid, but because of expanding local support for the movement. Giustozzi states that the Taliban have support among the clergy and have been good at exploiting local dissatisfactions and conflicts to win more recruits. Giustozzi concludes that winning a war against the Taliban will be extremely difficult.*

As you read, consider the following questions:

1. According to Giustozzi, why have the Taliban suffered high casualties and turned to improvised explosive devices?

Antonio Giustozzi, "The Resurgence of the Neo-Taliban," *OpenDemocracy.net*, December 15, 2007. Reproduced by permission.

2. As Giustozzi observes, who are the first to join the Taliban other than the clergy?

3. What is the principal political objective of the Taliban, according to Giustozzi?

The re-emergence of the neo-Taliban [a radical Islamic movement that governed Afghanistan from 1996–2001 and has fought an insurgency against the Afghan government since 2004] in Afghanistan is hardly breaking news, but the reasons for its spreading influence in the last two years [2006 and 2007] have rarely been reported, much less explained. Until 2006, its campaign was confined largely to the Pashtun [an Afghan ethic group from which most of the Taliban are drawn] heartland south of the Hindu Kush mountains, but as of late 2007 it has established communication—and supply lines in the west, north and northeast of the country, through which are being channelled fighters and munitions in order to open new fronts against international forces.

Western observers have been puzzled how the neo-Taliban has encroached on areas inhabited mainly by ethnic minorities, where traditionally they have been viewed as a Pashtun movement and received lukewarm support—at best. This [viewpoint] attempts a provisional answer to this question. . . .

Strategic Limitations

The neo-Taliban's achievement in widening its sphere of influence is all the more remarkable given that the movement's fighters are recklessly brave—a fact remarked on by coalition troops—but tactically often naïve. This explains why they have suffered high casualties and turned to improvised explosive devices (IEDs [homemade bombs often used in terrorist attacks or guerrilla warfare]) as "force multipliers". From 2005, the movement also resorted to suicide bombings, although these have more of a psychological than a strategic impact.

Contrary to a widespread view among Afghans, therefore, military proficiency is not the key to the neo-Taliban's success.

The movement is more technologically accomplished than hitherto and its media-savvy propaganda campaigns utilise DVDs and other formerly detested symbols of Western influence. And while some field commanders now rely on laptops to track logistics and casualties and help plan attacks, technical illiteracy among rank-and-file fighters continues to hamper its campaign, ruling out the effective deployment of anti-tank and anti-aircraft weapons.

External support—from foreign *jihadists* [fighters inspired by Islamic ideology or visions of Muslim freedom or brotherhood], from Pakistan and now possibly (on a much smaller scale) from Iran—is another oft-cited explanation of the neo-Taliban's resurgence, as is its (usually overestimated) involvement in the opium trade. However, these factors alone would not have allowed the neo-Taliban to become anything more than cross-border nuisance-raiders: entrenched support from among the wider Afghan population has also been required.

Winning Converts

While travelling in the north of Afghanistan recently I discovered that its modus operandi [method of procedure] mirrors that employed in the south, namely recruiting core fighters and propagandists from among the many Afghans living in Pakistan who are sympathetic to its aims. The latter travel deep inside Afghanistan, seeking potential recruits and mobilising support. They rely primarily on conservative clerical networks, mostly Deobandi-influenced [an Islamic methodology influential among the Taliban] for practical and motivational support. It is difficult to estimate how much backing the neo-Taliban enjoys among the clergy, but many of them [that is, the clergy] seem to look forward to the return to power of Mullah Omar [leader of Afghanistan from 1996–2001, and leader of the Taliban movement], under whose regime they

The Taliban Are Prepared to Fight On

Taliban militants said on Wednesday [December 2009] that the exit plan set by US President Barack Obama was a trick to appease the American public, and vowed that they were prepared to face the additional 30,000 US troops expected to arrive by next summer [2010]. . . .

[The Taliban Web site stated that] Taliban fighters were prepared to face the additional US and other NATO [North Atlantic Treaty Organization] troops "in all parts of the country."

Farhad Peikar,
"Roundup: Taliban Says Ready
to Face New US Troops in Afghanistan,"
Deutsche Presse-Agentur, December 2, 2009.

enjoyed unprecedented influence, locally and nationally. Certainly, hostility towards foreigners predominates among the *mullahs* [Islamic religious leaders], who often feel that Afghanistan is moving away from their own interpretation of Islam and that their role in society is diminishing.

Moreover, the support of the clergy alone would not have gotten the neo-Taliban very far; it was also essential that the mullahs acted as an intelligence network, reporting on village-level developments, thereby allowing the movement to identify and exploit opportunities to expand its recruitment. Throughout many areas the movement has courted disgruntled, disenfranchised and marginalised individuals and communities, which are often alienated by a dysfunctional system of remote-control government from Kabul [the capital and Afghanistan's largest city] in which cronyism and corruption drive provincial appointments.

The first to join the neo-Taliban (the clergy itself apart) are often socially marginal elements such as petty criminals, bandits and the young unemployed. But mass support has only been built where the movement has won over entire communities—as happened first in the Kandahar [the second largest city in Afghanistan] region, then increasingly among the southeastern and eastern Pashtuns. This has allowed the neo-Taliban to expand its ranks (my estimate is that it has now more than 20,000 men under arms). There is a high casualty rate, though community-mobilisation mechanisms mean that family members take the place of fallen fighters.

There are signs that this pattern is being replicated in the west and parts of northern Afghanistan, particularly within Pashtun pockets, which exist in almost every northern province. The big question now is whether the Taliban will win over Tajiks and Uzbeks [ethnic groups in Afghanistan]. While the presence of many pro-Taliban Tajik and Uzbek clerics is well attested, how will local communities respond to further incursions by the movement? The neo-Taliban is assiduously attempting to overcome the widely held perception that it is a Pashtun movement, hostile to minorities. Its skill in exploiting provincial grievances and conflicts cannot be underestimated.

No Good Solutions

Should negotiations with the neo-Taliban be considered as part of a solution to the conflict? Time seems to be on the movement's hands, given that the Canadian and Dutch governments among others are keen to reduce their involvement. The movement's principal objective remains a Deobandi re-Islamisation of Afghanistan. Despite many reports to the contrary, neither broader notions of Afghan nationalism nor ethnic politics drives the neo-Taliban leadership, although they may still influence its middle- and lower-ranking cadres.

The neo-Taliban has two non-negotiable demands: the withdrawal of all foreign troops and a greater role for religious law in framing Afghanistan's legal and social structures. For this reason a power-sharing agreement would achieve what many in the West want—disengagement—but at the price of risking a new phase of anarchy. A compromise agreement [would] be difficult to negotiate and (even if it were concluded) unlikely to last long. Some external observers, particularly in Pakistan, suggest that the only way to cut a deal might be via a move towards greater decentralisation or federalism in Afghanistan; this, they argue, would allow divergent views of how to run Afghanistan to coexist, and different factions and strongmen to exercise influence. The situation is poised between a war difficult to win and an unlikely peace.

> *"I believe we have fundamentally the right strategy in place, but even if that is so it will take some time to show progress."*

The Taliban Are Not Winning in Afghanistan

Gregor Peter Schmitz and Jeremy Shapiro

Interviewer Gregor Peter Schmitz is a reporter for the German newspaper Der Spiegel; *Jeremy Shapiro is the director of research at the Center on the United States and Europe at the Brookings Institution. In the following viewpoint, Shapiro argues that the Taliban have little support in Afghanistan and little capacity to fight Western troops. Thus, militarily, he contends, U.S. forces are doing well, though political issues and corruption in the Afghan government must be addressed. He concludes that more troops may be helpful, but that other issues are more important.*

As you read, consider the following questions:

1. According to Shapiro, how long will the U.S. and coalition forces need to commit to Afghanistan?

2. What problem does Shapiro say needs to be solved before asymmetric attacks in various parts of Afghanistan can be halted?

3. According to Shapiro, what European policy might be a disaster for NATO?

S piegel Online: *Policy makers in the US and Europe are shocked by the gloomy Pentagon assessment for Afghanistan. You, however, are pleading for more optimism. Why?*

[Jeremy] Shapiro: There is ample reason for gloom, but we need to keep in mind that in the best of circumstances, Afghanistan is a long-term mission. We are talking about a commitment of 10 or 20 years. I believe we have fundamentally the right strategy in place, but even if that is so, it will take some time to show progress. I don't believe we need the major review people are talking about.

More Soldiers Is Not the Answer

Everyone seems to be asking for more troops in Afghanistan, though. President George W. Bush, John McCain, even Barack Obama.[1]

More soldiers could be put to good use there, but they wouldn't fundamentally change the situation. Let's assume we would send in 10,000 more, as is contemplated: They could improve the local situation in a few areas for a time, but they would not rectify the problem of the Pakistani border areas and their ability to infiltrate insurgents into Afghanistan. As long as we don't solve that problem, you could put 100,000 soldiers into Afghanistan and you would still have asymmetric attacks in various parts of Afghanistan and a rate of civilian and military casualties similar to the current one. And I have not yet heard viable suggestions on how to deal with the problem of the Pakistani border areas.

1. John McCain was the Republican presidential candidate in 2008, when this article appeared. Barack Obama was the Democratic presidential candidate and later was elected U.S. president.

But isn't it understandable that security is paramount to people in Afghanistan?

Of course, but we can't solve that problem simply by increasing forces. Achieving overall security in Afghanistan will be a slow process and unfortunately, we will have to tolerate violence in the country for a long time. The insurgents are not winning in Afghanistan—they have no capacity to stand toe-to-toe with Western forces or the Afghan National Army. Their ideology is bankrupt and they are unpopular in the country. The real problem is the lack of civilian capacity in the international forces, corruption, and the dearth of effective Afghan governance capacity and security forces. These are actually harder issues to address than troop levels, but they must be tackled. Relatively speaking, the military part is actually in fairly good shape.

Then why is the debate so focused on a possible troop increase?

In political circles, we tend to avoid discussing the really tough issues—such as government reforms in Afghanistan. Instead, we do what we know: We throw more military forces at the problem. But what we really need is patience. That is something we have in very short supply in North American and European capitals. The current counterinsurgency strategy in Afghanistan is not a bad one. It takes time but there are signs of progress. Just look at the state of the Afghan National Army. Nearly everybody I talked to in Afghanistan raves about the army. It is adding about 4,000 people a month. They have not lost an encounter with insurgents since April of last year [2007].

Change the Terms of the Debate

That means the current debate on troop increases is wrongheaded?

I have mixed feelings about the debate. More attention for Afghanistan is certainly a good thing. But the debate seems

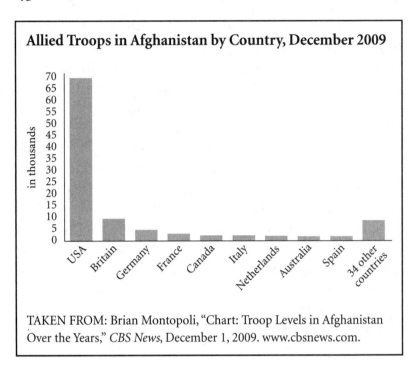

Allied Troops in Afghanistan by Country, December 2009

in thousands

70
65
60
55
50
45
40
35
30
25
20
15
10
5
0

USA Britain Germany France Canada Italy Netherlands Australia Spain 34 other countries

TAKEN FROM: Brian Montopoli, "Chart: Troop Levels in Afghanistan Over the Years," *CBS News*, December 1, 2009. www.cbsnews.com.

too influenced by comparisons with the surge in Iraq. There, increase in troops indeed dampened the violence. But if you look closer, one could observe in Iraq not just an increase of US troops but also a change of military strategy and a switch of tribal loyalties. The situation is simply not comparable with Afghanistan.

So would you advise Europeans to reject American demands for more troops?

Beyond the number of total Western forces in Afghanistan, there is also a trans-Atlantic question here. How should the trans-Atlantic partners share the burdens of the mission that has UN [United Nations] approval, that flies the NATO [North Atlantic Treaty Organization, a military alliance including the U.S. and Western European nations] flag, and that is supported by the vast majority of Afghans? Currently, the balance of commitment is skewed. If Europeans don't address that imbalance, the United States will probably continue to fill the gap. This would not be a disaster for Afghanistan, but it might be for NATO.

Would there be enough public support from Americans who are simply tired of the war effort?

Yes. Afghanistan is, unlike the Iraq invasion, a very bipartisan war. It is still very popular in the US—and there is a growing feeling that the conflict has been neglected.

"*Many observers have noted that there are no purely military solutions in Afghanistan. That is correct. Nonetheless, military action, while not sufficient by itself, is absolutely necessary.*"

The United States Must Increase Its Military Presence in Afghanistan

General David H. Petraeus

David H. Petraeus is a U.S. general and commander of the U.S. Central Command; he served as the commander overseeing coalition forces in Iraq. In the following viewpoint, he argues that it is important for the United States to remain in Afghanistan to prevent the nation from becoming a terrorist stronghold. He suggests committing more troops and resources to the effort, as well as recommitting to counterinsurgency efforts. He also argues that the United States must act in concert with local groups and must be aboveboard in its actions to win the trust of the Afghan people.

General David H. Petraeus, "The Future of the Alliance and the Mission in Afghanistan, presented at the 45th Munich Security Conference," nesa-center.org/node/239, February 8, 2009. Reproduced by permission.

As you read, consider the following questions:

1. When Petraeus says that Afghanistan needs more enablers, about what specific groups or equipment is he talking?

2. According to Petraeus, what is the decisive terrain in Afghanistan?

3. What examples does Petraeus give of ways in which U.S. forces need to stay true to their values?

This morning's [February 8, 2009] topic is Afghanistan, which Secretary of Defense [Robert] Gates recently described to the US Congress as posing "our greatest military challenge right now." As he noted, our fundamental objective in Afghanistan is to ensure that transnational terrorists are not able to reestablish the sanctuaries they enjoyed prior to 9/11 [September 11, 2001, when terrorists hijacked airplanes and crashed them into major US buildings]. It was to eliminate such sanctuaries that we took [military] action in Afghanistan in 2001. And preventing their reestablishment remains an imperative today—noting, to be sure, that achievement of that objective inevitably requires accomplishment of other interrelated tasks as well. And, President [Barack] Obama has directed a strategy review that will sharpen the clarity of those tasks.

Afghanistan Is a Difficult Mission

Afghanistan has been a very tough endeavor. Certainly, there have been important achievements there over the past seven years [since 2001]—agreement on a constitution, elections, and establishment of a government; increased access to education, health care, media, and telecommunications; construction of a significant number of infrastructure projects; development of the Afghan National Army; and others.

But in recent years the resurgence of the Taliban [an Afghan radical Islamic movement that controlled the country until 2001, and has since mounted an insurgency against the government] and al Qaeda [an international terrorist organization with links to the Taliban] has led to an increase in violence, especially in the southern and eastern parts of the country. Numerous other challenges have emerged as well, among them: difficulties in the development of governmental institutions that achieve legitimacy in the eyes of the Afghan people; corruption; expansion—until last year [2008]—of poppy production and the illegal narcotics industry; and difficulties in the establishment of the Afghan police.

In fact, there has been nothing easy about Afghanistan. And, as Senator [Joseph] Lieberman observed in a recent speech to the Brookings Institution, "Reversing Afghanistan's slide into insecurity will not come quickly, easily, or cheaply." Similarly, Secretary Gates told Congress, "This will undoubtedly be a long and difficult fight." I agree. In fact, I think it is important to be clear-eyed about the challenges that lie ahead, while also remembering the importance of our objectives in Afghanistan and the importance of the opportunity that exists if we all intensify our efforts and work together to achieve those objectives.

Many observers have noted that there are no purely military solutions in Afghanistan. That is correct. Nonetheless, military action, while not sufficient by itself, is absolutely necessary, for security provides the essential foundation for the achievement of progress in all the other so-called lines of operation—recognizing, of course, that progress in other areas made possible by security improvements typically contributes to further progress in the security arena—creating an upward spiral in which improvements in one area reinforce progress in another.

Arresting and then reversing the downward spiral in security in Afghanistan thus will require not just additional military forces, but also more civilian contributions, greater unity of effort between civilian and military elements and with our

Afghan partners, and a comprehensive approach, as well as sustained commitment and a strategy that addresses the situations in neighboring countries.

This morning, I'd like to describe in very general terms the resource requirements that are under discussion in Washington and various other national capitals. Then I'll describe briefly a few of the ideas that helped us in Iraq and that, properly adapted for Afghanistan, can help guide [General David D.] McKiernan [commander of forces in Afghanistan from October 2008 to June 2009] and ISAF [International Security Assistance Force].

More Forces Are Needed

In recent months, our president and many others have highlighted the need for additional forces in Afghanistan to reverse the downward spiral in security, help Afghan forces provide security for the elections on August 20th [2009], and enable progress in the tasks essential to achievement of our objectives. Indeed, as has been announced in recent months, more US forces are entering operations ... as part of ISAF in Afghanistan now, more have been ordered to deploy, and the deployment of others is under consideration. Beyond that, the number of Afghan soldiers to be trained and equipped has been increased, and many of the other troop-contributing nations will deploy additional forces, as well, with a number of commitments under discussion. And I would be remiss if I did not ask individual countries to examine what forces and other contributions they can provide as ISAF intensifies its efforts in preparation for the elections in August.

It is, of course not just additional combat forces that are required. ISAF also needs more so-called enablers to support the effort in Afghanistan—more intelligence, surveillance, and reconnaissance platforms and the connectivity to exploit the capabilities they bring; more military, police, engineers, and logistics elements; additional special operations forces and civil affairs units; more lift and attack helicopters and fixed-wing aircraft; additional air medevac assets; increases in information operations capabilities; and so on. Also required are more Embedded Training Teams, Operational Mentor and Liaison Teams, and Police Mentoring Teams, all elements that are essential to building capable Afghan National Security Forces. And I applaud the German Defense Minister's announcement of additional police and army training teams this morning. As with combat forces, some additional enabler elements are already flowing to Afghanistan, commitments have been made to provide others, and others are under discussion as well. As Senator Lieberman highlighted in his Brookings speech, a surge in civilian capacity is needed to match the increase in military forces in order to field adequate numbers of provincial reconstruction teams and other civilian elements—teams and personnel that are essential to help our Afghan partners expand their capabilities in key governmental areas, to support basic economic development, and to assist in the development of various important aspects of the rule of law, including initiatives to support the development of police and various judicial initiatives.

It is also essential, of course, that sufficient financial resources be provided for the effort in Afghanistan. It is hugely important that nations deliver on pledges of economic development assistance, that the Afghan National Army and Law and Order Trust Fund [for Afghanistan] be fully financed, that support be maintained for the Afghanistan Reconstruction Trust Fund, and that resources continue to be provided for the projects conducted by our military units and PRTs [Provincial Reconstruction Teams] at local levels. And, I applaud the German Defense Minister's announcement of additional development aid this morning, too.

Of course, just more troops, civilians, dollars and euros won't be enough. As students of history, we're keenly aware that Afghanistan has, over the years, been known as the grave-

Petraeus's Iraq and Afghanistan Strategy

General David Petraeus, who commanded the surge in Iraq, was recommended April 23 [2008] by U.S. Secretary of Defense Robert Gates to be the next head of U.S. Central Command (CENTCOM). . . . This means Petraeus would remain in ultimate command of the war in Iraq while also taking command in Afghanistan. . . .

In Iraq, Petraeus changed the nature of the war. The change he brought to bear there was not so much military as political. Certainly, he deployed his forces differently than his predecessors, dispersing some of them in small units based in villages and neighborhoods contested by insurgents. That was not a trivial change, but it was not as important as the process of political discussions he began with local leaders.

George Friedman,
"Petraeus, Afghanistan and the Lessons of Iraq,"
STRATFOR, May 6, 2008. www.stratfor.com.

yard of empires. It is, after all, a country that has never taken kindly to outsiders bent on conquering it. We cannot take that history lightly. And our awareness of it should caution us to recognize that, while additional forces are essential, their effectiveness will depend on how they are employed, as that, in turn, will determine how they are seen by the Afghan population.

Counterinsurgency in Afghanistan

What I'd like to discuss next, then, are some of the concepts that our commanders have in mind as plans are refined to employ additional forces. I base this on discussions with Gen.

McKiernan and others who have served in Afghanistan, as well as on lessons learned in recent years. I do so with awareness that a number of the elements on the ground are operating along the lines of these ideas—and that their ability to do so will be enhanced by the increased density on the ground of ISAF and Afghan forces as additional elements deploy to the most challenging areas. Counterinsurgency operations are, after all, troop intensive. Finally, I want to underscore the fact that commanders on the ground will, as always, operationalize the so-called big ideas in ways that are appropriate for their specific situations on the ground. So here are some of those ideas:

First and foremost, our forces and those of our Afghan partners have to strive to secure and serve the population. We have to recognize that the Afghan people are the decisive "terrain." And together with our Afghan partners, we have to work to provide the people [with] security, to give them respect, to gain their support, and to facilitate the provision of basic services, the development of the Afghan [National] Security Forces in the area, the promotion of local economic development, and the establishment of governance that includes links to the traditional leaders in society and is viewed as legitimate in the eyes of the people. Securing and serving the people requires that our forces be good neighbors. While it may be less culturally acceptable to live among the people in certain parts of Afghanistan than it was in Iraq, it is necessary to locate Afghan and ISAF forces where they can establish a persistent security presence. You can't commute to work in the conduct of counterinsurgency operations. Positioning outposts and patrol bases, then, requires careful thought, consultation with local leaders, and the establishment of good local relationships to be effective.

Positioning near those we and our Afghan partners are helping to secure also enables us to understand the neighborhood. A nuanced appreciation of the local situation is essential. Leaders and troopers have to understand the tribal structures, the power brokers, the good guys and the bad guys, local cultures and history, and how systems are supposed to work and do work. This requires listening and being respectful of local elders and mullahs [Islamic religious leaders], and farmers and shopkeepers—and it also requires, of course, many cups of tea.

It is also essential that we achieve unity of effort, that we coordinate and synchronize the actions of all ISAF and Afghan forces—and those of our Pakistani partners across the border—and that we do the same with the actions of our embassy and international partners, our Afghan counterparts, local governmental leaders, and international and nongovernmental organizations. Working to a common purpose is essential in the conduct of counterinsurgency operations.

We also, in support of and in coordination with our Afghan partners, need to help promote local reconciliation, although this has to be done very carefully and in accordance with the principles established in the Afghan Constitution. In concert with and in support of our Afghan partners, we need to identify and separate the "irreconcilables" from the "reconcilables," striving to create the conditions that can make the reconcilables part of the solution, even as we kill, capture, or drive out the irreconcilables. In fact, programs already exist in this area and careful application of them will be essential in the effort to fracture and break off elements of the insurgency in order to get various groups to put down their weapons and support the legitimate Constitution of Afghanistan.

Having said that, we must pursue the enemy relentlessly and tenaciously. True irreconcilables, again, must be killed, captured, or driven out of the area. And we cannot shrink from that any more than we can shrink from being willing to support Afghan reconciliation with those elements that show a willingness to reject the insurgents and help Afghan and ISAF forces.

Establishing Legitimacy

To ensure that the gains achieved endure, ISAF and Afghan forces have to hold areas that have been cleared. Once we fight to clear and secure an area, we must ensure that it is retained. The people—and local security forces—need to know that we will not abandon them. Additionally, we should look for ways to give local citizens a stake in the success of the local security effort and in the success of the new Afghanistan more broadly as well. To this end, a reformed, capable Afghan National Police force—with the necessary support from the international community and the alliance—is imperative to ensuring the ability to protect the population. And the new Afghan Population Protection Program announced by MOI [Minister of the Interior Mohammad] Atmar holds considerable promise and deserves our support as well.

On a related note, to help increase the legitimacy of the Afghan government, we need to help our Afghan partners give the people a reason to support the government and their local authorities. This includes helping enable Afghan solutions to Afghan problems. And on a related note, given the importance of Afghan solutions and governance being viewed as legitimate by the people and in view of allegations of corruption, such efforts likely should feature support for what might be called an "Afghan accountability offensive" as well. That will be an important effort.

In all that we do as we perform various missions, we need to live our values. While our forces should not hesitate to engage and destroy an enemy, our troopers must also stay true to the values we hold dear. This is, after all, an important element that distinguishes us from the enemy, and it manifests itself in many ways, including making determined efforts to reduce to the absolute minimum civilian casualties—an effort furthered significantly by the tactical direction and partnering initiatives developed by Gen. McKiernan with our Afghan counterparts.

We also must strive to be first with the truth. We need to beat the insurgents and extremists to the headlines and to preempt rumors. We can do that by getting accurate information to the chain of command, to our Afghan partners, and to the press as soon as is possible. Integrity is critical to this fight. Thus, when situations are bad, we should freely acknowledge that fact and avoid temptations to spin. Rather, we should describe the setbacks and failures we suffer and then state what we've learned from them and how we'll adjust to reduce the chances of similar events in the future.

Finally, we always must strive to learn and adapt. The situation in Afghanistan has changed significantly in the past several years and it continues to evolve. This makes it incumbent on us to assess the situation continually and to adjust our plans, operations, and tactics as required. We should share good ideas and best practices, but we also should never forget that what works in an area today may not work there tomorrow, and that what works in one area may not work in another.

Afghanistan Remains Vital

In conclusion, allow me to reiterate the key points I've sought to make. We have a hugely important interest in ensuring that Afghanistan does not once again become a sanctuary for transnational terrorists. Achieving that core objective, in turn, requires the accomplishment of several other significant tasks. Although there have been impressive achievements in Afghanistan since 2001, the security situation has deteriorated markedly in certain areas in the past two years. Reversing that trend is necessary to improve security for the population, to permit the conduct of free and fair elections in August, and to enable progress in other important areas. Achieving security improvements will require more ISAF and Afghan security forces of all types—combat, combat support, logistics, trainers and advisors, special operations, and so on. Some additional forces are already deploying, further increases have been ordered or pledged, and more are under discussion. To be effective, the additional military forces will need to be employed in accordance with counterinsurgency concepts applied by leaders who have a nuanced understanding of their areas of operation. And to complement and capitalize on the increased military resources, more civilian assets, adequate financial resources, close civil-military cooperation, and a comprehensive approach that encompasses regional states will be necessary. None of this will be easy. Indeed, as Vice President [Joe] Biden observed recently, Afghanistan likely will get harder before it gets easier. And sustained progress will require sustained commitment. But, again, our objectives are of enormous importance, a significant opportunity is at hand, and we all need to summon the will and the resources necessary to make the most of it.

"In Afghanistan, the trouble has always been getting out, not in."

The United States Should Not Send More Troops to Afghanistan

H.D.S. Greenway

H.D.S. Greenway is a foreign affairs columnist for the Boston Globe. *In the following viewpoint, he argues that invaders trying to take over Afghanistan have historically met with exhaustion and defeat. He also compares Afghanistan to Vietnam and suggests that the insurgency will grow more popular as more U.S. troops enter the country. He concludes that the United States should keep some forces in Afghanistan to prevent the return of terrorist groups such as al Qaeda but should not increase troop numbers.*

As you read, consider the following questions:

1. During the period known as the Great Game, why did Britain invade Afghanistan, in the author's view?

H.D.S. Greenway, "No More Troops to Afghanistan," *The Boston Globe*, September 22, 2009. Copyright © 2009 Globe Newspaper Company. Reproduced by permission of the author.

2. What does Greenway see as the problem with a pacification program designed to protect the population of Afghanistan?

3. According to Greenway, what is the loya jirga or shura?

O n an autumn night in 1415, in their anxiety-filled camp on the "vasty fields of France," the English waited for the dawn that would bring them to battle at Agincourt "upon St. Crispin's day."

The king's generals feared they could not win without more troops. [Playwright William] Shakespeare has the earl of Westmoreland say [in *Henry V*]: "O that we now had here/ But one ten thousand of those men in England/ That do no work today!"

But [King] Henry V answers: "No my fair cousin . . . God's will I pray thee, wish not one man more."

The king, in the most memorable call to war in all literature, says he does not want his "happy few," his "band of brothers," to have to share the glory, but the truth was he hadn't more troops to spare.

Afghanistan Compared with Vietnam

Henry's admonishment to the earl was recalled some five-and-a-half centuries after Agincourt when another general, William Westmoreland, wanted to throw more soldiers into Vietnam. He, too, was turned down.

With General Stanley A. McChrystal's report calling for additional troops now public, President [Barack] Obama will soon have his King Henry moment: whether or not to send more troops into the ever-worsening war in Afghanistan. Much depends on his definition of the mission. Is it to defeat the Taliban [the Islamic extremist movement leading the insurgency in Afghanistan] in battle as Henry defeated the flower of French chivalry? There will be no famous victories in the irregular warfare that has so marked Afghanistan over the centuries.

Is it to create a viable, democratic, centralized state on a Western model? When he came to power, Obama seemed to realize that the mission of his predecessor, George W. Bush, was too ambitious and that he should settle for simply making Afghanistan inhospitable to al Qaeda [the terrorist group linked to the September 11, 2001, attacks on the United States]. In the meantime, however, "mission creep"—the tendency of any mission to expand and grow if it is not carefully pruned—has been the order of the day. Obama runs the risk of turning Afghanistan into a full-fledged dependency of the United States.

Recently, when asked if he risked the fate of Lyndon Johnson whose presidency was consumed by a war started by his predecessors, but which he chose to reinforce, Obama replied: "You have to learn lessons from history. On the other hand, each historical moment is different. You never step into the same river twice. And so Afghanistan is not Vietnam."

Afghanistan may not be Vietnam, but it has its own river of history that Obama is stepping into. Centuries of conquerors have found that river too swift and the currents too confusing to navigate.

In the 19th century, the British, having conquered India, looked upon Afghanistan "as a menace, shadowy, but none the less formidable to the peace and security of their North Western territories," as [British official] W.K. Fraser-Tytler wrote 60 years ago. The description could fit America's view of Afghanistan if you substitute North America for North Western territories. But it wasn't so much the threat of Afghan hordes pouring through the Khyber Pass [a mountain pass linking Pakistan and Afghanistan] that finally alarmed the British. It was political disintegration and chaos in Afghanistan at the time. Who might fill the vacuum?

Afghanistan Has Defeated Many Invasions

For 200 years the essential fact about Western intervention in Afghanistan has been fear of what other foreigners might do there, not Afghanistan itself.

In the period known as the "Great Game," [the period between 1813–1917 when Britain and Russia vied for influence in Central Asia] it was Britain's fear of Russian influence that led it to invade Afghanistan, often with disastrous results. In 1842 it lost an entire army, save one man, and was still intervening in Afghan affairs until well into the 20th century. The British were dropping bombs in Kabul [the capital of Afghanistan] as late as 1919.

When the Russians fulfilled Britain's nightmare and invaded Afghanistan in 1979 to ensure a pro-Soviet regime, the Americans took up the Great Game, arming holy warriors to harry the Russians out. It took nine years before the defeated Russians left, and Afghanistan sank back into chaos.

In this century it was another group of foreigners, this time the mostly Arab al Qaeda, that brought Afghanistan to the world's attention. The Americans invaded because of al Qaeda and 9/11, not because of Afghanistan.

Obama may have been right that Afghanistan was a war of necessity after 9/11, and he was certainly right that Iraq was an unnecessary diversion. But that was 2001, and al Qaeda leaders were allowed to slip away into Pakistan, where it has proved impossible to find them, much less destroy them. Eight years later, al Qaeda no longer needs Afghanistan. It's better off in Pakistan.

As it was for the British and the Russians before them, Americans found invading Afghanistan was a pushover. In Afghanistan, the trouble has always been getting out, not in.

The capital, Kabul, was not liberated from the Taliban by American tanks, but by Afghans of the Northern Alliance. When I visited the country in 2003, the Afghans did not feel like an occupied people. But as the American footprint grows larger and heavier, and as civilian casualties mount, Secretary of Defense Robert Gates isn't alone in worrying that the United States will be seen more and more as an occupying power.

America's new strategy focuses on protecting the population, which is all well and good, but a pacification program as envisioned will cost billions, take decades, and even then might not work.

In 30 years of war, Afghanistan is much worse off now in terms of literacy and social cohesion than it was before. There are few institutions on which to build a stable democracy. Afghanistan is a tribal society in which people feel less connected to the state than their own local leaders. We see the Taliban as bad and government forces as good. But Afghans see Tajiks with perhaps too much power in the capital, Uzbeks and Hazaras too with their own interests, while Pashtuns, who form the largest group, feel somewhat disenfranchised. Too many Pashtuns see the Taliban as representing their interests.

More Troops Will Increase Resentment

Americans disapprove of warlords because we want to see the state have a monopoly on violence, but to many Afghans, warlords are tribal, regional, and ethnic leaders for whom loyalty seems more deserving than the government in Kabul.

The recent and ludicrously corrupt elections [in August 2009] show how hard it will be to instill a sense of what we call democracy for those who say that the traditional loya jirga, or shura, a meeting of tribal elders, is a better way of expressing government by the people and of the people than our style of elections.

When you commit ever more troops to a theater, "force protection"—the need to protect your own soldiers—becomes a dominant factor regardless of what those soldiers were supposed to achieve by being there. You could hear this in Sena-

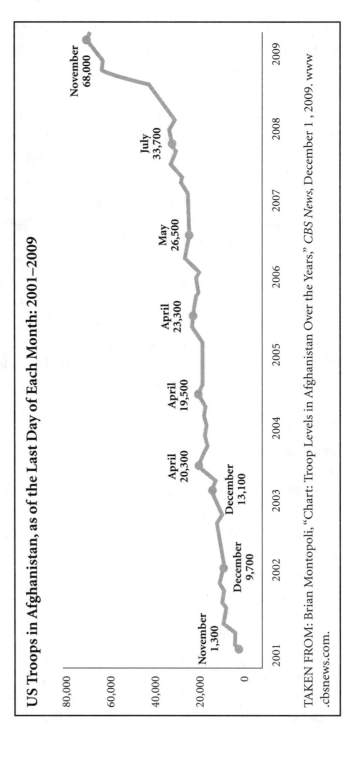

US Troops in Afghanistan, as of the Last Day of Each Month: 2001–2009

November 1,300

December 9,700

December 13,100

April 20,300

April 19,500

April 23,300

May 26,500

July 33,700

November 68,000

80,000

60,000

40,000

20,000

0

2001   2002   2003   2004   2005   2006   2007   2008   2009

TAKEN FROM: Brian Montopoli, "Chart: Troop Levels in Afghanistan Over the Years," *CBS News*, December 1, 2009. www .cbsnews.com.

tor [John] McCain's statement that failure to send more troops would put "young American lives in danger."

But when Admiral Mike Mullen, chairman of the Joint Chiefs of Staff, was asked if Afghans could stand on their own, his answer was: "No, sir." One has to ask why, after eight years, our Afghans cannot stand up to the Taliban, any more than Russia's Afghans could stand up to the mujahideen [freedom fighters] in the 1980s.

For that matter, why could our Vietnamese not stand up to [Communist revolutionary and president of Vietnam] Ho Chi Minh's Vietnamese? Could it be that our Afghans are being increasingly perceived as puppets?

Obama should not abandon Afghanistan. International efforts to develop the country should continue, and force levels should be kept to the level necessary to keep al Qaeda from regaining a foothold.

But we stand at a crossroads. We can keep a sustainable military and civilian effort in play in Afghanistan, or we can basically take over the country and face down the growing civil and holy wars that have little to do with the reason we invaded Afghanistan in the first place. This decision is more important than the number of troops.

Rather than becoming the new Russians who found themselves hated foreigners, we should accept more modest goals.

The history of Afghanistan suggests that we are not equipped to make over the country to our liking, and the history of the United States suggests that Americans give up these efforts sooner rather than later.

King Henry had technology on his side at Agincourt. The long bow was the Predator Drone of its day. But Americans are not interested in hundred-year wars, which is what the English were engaged in on that St. Crispin's Day.

| *"The one issue that should be at the core of the United States' Afghan strategy is Pakistan. It is there, not Afghanistan, where the United States has vital national interests."*

The United States Should Focus on Pakistan, Not Afghanistan

Richard N. Haass

Richard N. Haass is the president of the Council on Foreign Relations and the author of War of Necessity, War of Choice: A Memoir of Two Iraq Wars. *In the following viewpoint, he argues that Pakistan, which has nuclear weapons and currently harbors terrorists, is much more important to U.S. interests than Afghanistan. Haass recommends concentrating U.S. troop presence in Afghanistan to major cities and substantially increasing aid to Pakistan. He also suggests that the U.S. goal in both countries should be moderate stability rather than actual peace and prosperity.*

As you read, consider the following questions:

1. According to Haass, what will terrorists do if they are prevented from using Afghanistan as a base?

2. The United States should coordinate Afghanistan policy in a high-level diplomatic group with which nations, in the author's view?

3. The United States needs to husband resources to confront threats from which nations, according to Haass?

Why does Afghanistan matter?

We generally hear four arguments. First, if the Taliban [a radical Islamic group that controlled Afghanistan from 1996–2001 and now leads the insurgency] returns to power, Afghanistan will again be a haven for terrorist groups. Second, if the Taliban takes over, Afghanistan will again become a human rights nightmare. Third, a perceived defeat of the United States in Afghanistan would be a blow to U.S. prestige everywhere and would embolden radicals. Fourth, an Afghanistan under Taliban control would be used by extremists as a sanctuary from which to destabilize Pakistan.

Afghanistan Is of Limited Importance

None of these assumptions is as strong as proponents maintain. Afghanistan certainly matters—the question is how much.

[Terrorist group] al Qaeda does not require Afghan real estate to constitute a regional or global threat. Terrorists gravitate to areas of least resistance; if they cannot use Afghanistan, they will use countries such as Yemen or Somalia, as in fact they already are. No doubt, the human rights situation would grow worse under Taliban rule, but helping Afghan girls get an education, no matter how laudable, is not a goal that justifies an enormous U.S. military commitment. And yes, the taking of Kabul [Afghanistan's capital] by the Taliban would become part of the radicals' narrative, but the United States fared well in Asia after the fall of South Vietnam, and less than a decade after an ignominious withdrawal from Beirut, the United States amassed the international coalition that ousted [former Iraqi leader] Saddam Hussein from Kuwait. There are and always will be opportunities to demonstrate the effectiveness of U.S. power.

The one issue that should be at the core of the United States' Afghan strategy is Pakistan. It is there, not Afghanistan, where the United States has vital national interests. These stem from Pakistan's dozens of nuclear weapons, the presence on its soil of the world's most dangerous terrorists and the potential for a clash with India that could escalate to a nuclear confrontation.

The United States is doing a great deal in Afghanistan—and is considering doing more—because it sees the effort as essential to protecting Pakistan. But this logic is somewhat bizarre. Certainly, allowing the Taliban and al Qaeda to reestablish a sanctuary in Afghanistan would make it harder to defeat them in Pakistan. But the Taliban and al Qaeda already have a sanctuary—in Pakistan itself.

It is the government of Pakistan that is tolerating the very groups that the United States is fighting in Afghanistan in the name of Pakistan's stability. It is worth noting, too, that Pakistani officials are not asking the United States to commit additional troops to Afghanistan, in large part because many Pakistanis view Afghanistan as one of several fronts in their struggle against India and see the Taliban as foot soldiers in that contest. Pakistan's future will be determined far more by its willingness and ability to meet internal challenges than by anything that emanates from across its border.

A War of Choice

All of this argues that U.S. interests in Afghanistan are less than fundamental, rendering the conflict not a war of necessity but a war of choice. As befitting a war of choice, there are options available to the United States that fall between sending tens of thousands of additional troops, as General Stanley McChrystal is reportedly requesting, and simply abandoning the country to its fate—options in which the costs and benefits are consistent with what is at stake.

Recent news accounts suggest that President [Barack] Obama is seeking precisely such a middle ground. What might it look like? The United States would maintain for now roughly its current number of troops in Afghanistan, although the balance between trainers and war fighters would shift toward the former. It would train the Afghan National Army and police force at an accelerated pace. Just as important, the United States would increase its arming and training of regional and local army and police forces loyal to selected local leaders. This would be akin to the successful strategy in the Sunni [a branch of Islam] areas of Iraq and would reflect the Afghan reality of a weak center coexisting with strong warlords. Over time, these steps would allow for a gradual reduction in U.S. forces.

The United States would spend money liberally to redirect the loyalty of individuals and groups tied to the Taliban. Many are Pashtun [an ethnic group in Afghanistan from which most members of the Taliban are drawn] nationalists more than anything else; there is no reason to assume that all Taliban members are implacably opposed to the United States or are committed to reestablishing the intimate ties with al Qaeda that they had a decade ago.

The United States would increase aid to the government in Kabul only if President Hamid Karzai agrees to form a broad-based coalition government. Without this, he will not have the legitimacy to lead—or to be an effective partner for the United States—given the fraud that characterized the recent national election [in August 2009].

U.S. and Afghan armed forces would be concentrated in the capital and major population areas. Drone attacks would be ordered when high-value targets were identified and the prospects for collateral damage were slight. A standing high-level diplomatic group involving Afghanistan's immediate neighbors (including Iran) and others with a stake in the country's future (the United States, Russia, India, Europe) would meet regularly to coordinate policy.

More for Pakistan

Aid to Pakistan would rise dramatically. It makes no sense that the United States now invests $20, or by some estimates $30, in Afghanistan for every $1 it spends in Pakistan. Pakistani textiles would gain easier access to the U.S. market. And the United States would expend greater diplomatic effort to reduce Indo-Pakistani tensions.

Would this strategy work? No, if by "work" one envisions Afghanistan and Pakistan as peaceful, prosperous and responsible states living side by side. But our goals need to be more modest. What the United States and the world should seek is a Pakistan that remains intact, and exercises tight control over its nuclear weapons and considerable if not total control over terrorists within its borders. In Afghanistan, the near-term goal should be the building of a central government that, together with various local leaders, can limit the presence of terrorists. Anyone who thinks this is not bold enough should keep in mind that even modest objectives tend to be ambitious in this part of the world.

It is an error to equate the depth of U.S. commitment to the level of combat troops, as greater numbers and activity will not necessarily lead to results commensurate with the cost. Aid must be generous but conditioned on commitments and performance, and military and economic costs must be kept in check. And it is essential to remember that Afghanistan is but one of the strategic challenges facing the United States. Resources must be husbanded for Iran, Iraq and North Korea, to name just a few. McChrystal has the responsibility to

Afghanistan and Pakistan Are Linked

The future of Afghanistan is inextricably linked to the future of its neighbor, Pakistan. In the nearly eight years since 9/11 [September 11, 2001, terrorist attacks on the United States], al Qaeda and its extremist allies have moved across the border to the remote areas of the Pakistani frontier. This almost certainly includes al Qaeda's leadership: Osama bin Laden and Ayman al-Zawahiri. They have used this mountainous terrain as a safe haven to hide, train terrorists, communicate with followers, plot attacks, and send fighters to support the insurgency in Afghanistan. For the American people, this border region has become the most dangerous place in the world.

But this is not simply an American problem—far from it. It is, instead, an international security challenge of the highest order. Terrorist attacks in London and [the Indonesian island] Bali were tied to al Qaeda and its allies in Pakistan, as were attacks in North Africa and the Middle East, in Islamabad [Pakistan's capital] and Kabul [Afghanistan's capital]. If there is a major attack on an Asian, European, or African city, it—too—is likely to have ties to al Qaeda's leadership in Pakistan. The safety of people around the world is at stake.

Barack Obama,
"President Obama's Speech on Afghanistan and Pakistan,"
US News & World Report, *March 27, 2009. www.usnews.com.*

argue for the resources he believes are needed to fulfill his mission in Afghanistan; the president, responsible for protecting U.S. interests worldwide, has no such luxury.

It has become fashionable to deride a middle way on tough policy challenges. Those in the center are deemed guilty of the sort of incrementalism that got us in trouble in Vietnam, indecisiveness or worse. In Afghanistan, however, it may be that a middle way between surging and leaving is the best—or more accurately, the least bad—option.

> *"No amount of experience, area exper-*
> *tise, or language skills can make US*
> *forces a substitute for local forces and*
> *the legitimacy they can bring."*

Afghan Security Forces Must Be Made Ready to Take over Military Responsibilities

Anthony H. Cordesman and Adam Mausner

Anthony H. Cordesman holds the Arleigh A. Burke Chair in Strategy at the Center for Strategic and International Studies (CSIS) and also acts as a national security analyst for ABC News. Adam Mausner is a research associate at CSIS. In the following viewpoint, they argue that U.S. success in Afghanistan will be predicated on increasing the size, readiness, and role of Afghan security forces. The authors note that much progress has been made, but warn that more resources must be committed and more attention paid to quality training, especially in the field, if the United States is to be successful in the war in Afghanistan.

Anthony H. Cordesman and Adam Mausner, "Afghan National Security Forces: Shaping Host Country Forces as Part of Armed Nation Building," CSIS.org, October 30, 2009. All content © copyright 2010 CSIS Center for Strategic and International Studies. Reproduced by permission.

As you read, consider the following questions:

1. According to the authors, the United States has failed to learn enough from previous advisory efforts in which countries?

2. In the authors' view, no other efforts toward victory will matter if the United States does not provide the Afghan people with what?

3. Training efforts in Afghanistan have been far-better funded, manned, and structured after what date, according to Cordesman and Mausner?

For all of the debate over the best strategy for Afghanistan, there is a broad consensus that Afghan National Security Forces need major improvements in force quality, should be rapidly expanded to something close to twice their current level, and need major reforms in partnering and in their ability to execute a population-centric strategy. . . .

[This viewpoint] shows that issues involved are necessarily complex, but that several things are clear. Afghanistan and Iraq have both shown that the United States must look far beyond the normal definition of counterinsurgency to determine how it can conduct armed nation building as a critical element of hybrid warfare. This requires an integrated civil-military effort in which providing lasting security for the population, and economic and political stability, will often be far more important than success in tactical engagements with enemy forces. It also requires the US to understand that important as its traditional allies are, the key ally will be the host country [in this case, Afghanistan] and not simply its government but its population.

Using Afghanistan's Forces

Shaping the full range of host country security forces—from armed forces to regular police—has already proven to be a critical element in building such an alliance. No amount of experience, area expertise, or language skills can make US forces a substitute for local forces and the legitimacy they can bring. The US cannot structure its forces to provide a lasting substitute for the scale of forces needed to defeat an insurgency deal with internal tensions and strife, and fight what will often be enduring conflicts.

No US efforts in strategic communications or aid can substitute for a host government's ability to both communicate with its own people and win legitimacy in ideological, religious, and secular terms. Key aspects of operations—winning popular support, obtaining human intelligence, minimizing civil casualties and collateral damage, and transitioning from military operations to a civil rule of law—all depend on both the quality and quantity of host country forces, and a level of partnership that assures the people of a host country that the US will put its government and forces in the lead as soon as possible—and will leave once a host country is stable and secure.

The US has taken more than a half a decade to learn these lessons in both Afghanistan and Iraq. It has made major progress in recent years, but its efforts remain deeply flawed and the US military as well as outside military analysts still have not learned many of the painful lessons of Vietnam, Lebanon, and previous advisory efforts. At the same time, a US "whole of government" integrated civil-military effort, and true civil-military joint campaign plan represent at best a work [in] progress and often are little more than a triumph of rhetoric over reality.

Some of the gravest problems lie on the civil side, and the failure of the State Department and the civil departments of government to develop the necessary operational capabilities even after more than eight years of war [starting in 2001]. The US military, however, has yet to demonstrate that it can effectively and objectively manage its efforts to develop host country forces in ways that honestly assess their progress, the trade-offs needed between quality and quantity, and the need to create partners, rather than adjunct or surrogate forces.

This is partly a failure at the formal training level—sometimes dictated by unrealistic efforts to accelerate force quantity without considering the real-world pace at which progress can occur. The pace of host nation force development can be slowed by a number of factors, including: national traditions and social values, the impact of a lack of political accommodation and capacity in the host country government, and the impact of ethnic, sectarian, and tribal divisions within the armed forces.

US Failures

There also, however, have been two chronic failures in US efforts.

One is the inability to properly structure efforts to create true partners once new units complete the formal training process and provide the proper quality and number of mentors, partner units, enablers, and efforts to integrate higher level command structures. Far too often, the US has also sought to rush new battalion-sized combat elements into service to meet its own short-term needs without considering the resulting problems in quality, force retention, and host country perceptions of the result. Expediency has led to fundamentally misleading ratings of unit warfighting capability ..., using up half-prepared forces in combat, and major leadership and retention problems.

The other is a series of far more drastic failures to create effective police and security forces. These include the failure to properly assess the need for paramilitary police that can operate in a hostile counterinsurgency environment; the need to structure other police and security elements in ways that suit the constraints imposed by a lack of government

Canadian Objectives for the Afghan National Security Forces

By 2011, Canada expects that the ANA [Afghan National Army] in Kandahar [Afghanistan] will demonstrate an increased capacity to conduct operations and sustain a more secure environment in key districts of Kandahar, with support from ISAF [International Security Assistance Force] allies. Canada also expects the Afghan National Police (ANP) will demonstrate an increased capacity to promote law and order in key districts of Kandahar, supported by justice-sector and corrections capabilities.

Benchmarks to measure Afghan National Army progress are very precise and consistent with NATO's [North Atlantic Treaty Organization's] overall ANA training initiatives. To strengthen the policing, justice and corrections sectors, our benchmarks include both quantitative and qualitative indicators. A number of external factors will affect our ability to make progress in these areas. Insurgent violence deliberately targeting Afghan police has resulted in high rates of death, injury and desertion, which degrade police effectiveness and limit our ability to track trained police officers. Canada is one of many actors contributing to rule-of-law reform: Afghan ministries are leading this process and key international partners are playing critical roles.

Government of Canada,
"Priority 1: Training and Mentoring
Afghan National Security Forces,"
September 15, 2009. www.afghanistan.gc.ca.

capacity, corruption, differing cultural values; and the need to create a "rule of law" or civil order based on host country standards rather than US or Western values.

The US will lose the war in Afghanistan unless it makes far more effective efforts to correct these problems in what now seems likely to be an effort to accelerate training to reaching current force goals while doubling the overall size of the force. Military action is only a part of the strategy needed to win in Afghanistan, but no other effort towards victory will matter if the Afghan people cannot be given enough security and stability to allow successful governance, the opportunity for development, and an established civil society and rule of law that meets Afghan needs and expectations.

The creation of more effective host country forces is critical to achieving these ends. NATO/ISAF [North Atlantic Treaty Organization/International Security Assistance Force] and US forces cannot hope to win a military victory on their own. Their success will be determined in large part by how well and how quickly they build up a much larger and more effective Afghan National Security Forces (ANSF) first to support NATO/ISAF efforts, then take the lead, and eventually replace NATO/ISAF and US forces.

No meaningful form of success can occur, however, without giving the development of ANSF forces a much higher priority. . . .

Recent planning efforts indicate that such an effort must nearly double the ANA [Afghan National Army] and ANP [Afghan National Police] although early success could make full implementation of such plans unnecessary. Making a fully resourced start will ensure that adequate ANSF forces will be available over time, and greatly ease the strain of maintaining and increasing NATO/ISAF forces. Funding such expansion to the ANSF will also be far cheaper than maintaining or increasing NATO/ISAF forces.

Careful Expansion

But, such efforts must not race beyond either Afghan or US/NATO/ISAF capabilities. Quality will often be far more important than quantity, and enduring ANSF capability far more important than generating large initial force strengths. US/NATO/ISAF expediency cannot be allowed to put half-ready and unstable units in the field. It cannot be allowed to push force expansion efforts faster than ANSF elements can absorb them or the US/NATO/ISAF can provide fully qualified trainers, mentors, and partner units and the proper mix of equipment, facilities, enablers, and sustainability.

US/NATO/ISAF expediency cannot afford to ignore the impact of Afghan cultural needs, regional and ethnic differences, family and tribal structures, and the real-world "friction" that affects force development. Slogans and rhetoric about ideological goals, leadership, and morale cannot be allowed to lead the force development effort to ignore Afghan material realities: problems in pay, corruption, problems in promotion, inadequate facilities and equipment, poor medical care, overstretching or over-committing force elements, problems in supporting families, vulnerability to insurgent infiltration and threats, and a lack of meaningful compensation for death and disability. The US military and NATO/ISAF have systematically ignored such problems in the past, and understated or lied about their impact.

It may be conceptually attractive to compare the price of creating Afghan forces to those of deploying US and NATO/ISAF forces. It is certainly clear that the US and NATO/ISAF cannot or will not deploy and sustain the forces necessary to compensate for any failure to expand Afghan forces. It will be a disaster, however, if the real-world problems in creating truly effective ANSF partners are not fully addressed and equal attention is not given to correcting these problems. Each problem is a way to lose, and force expansion that fails to solve them cannot be a way to win.

They also need to realize that improvements in the training base are needed. . . . At the same time, no element of the ANSF can simply be trained and thrust into operations. Moreover, the key to success is not the quality of the training in training centers, but the quality of the partnering, mentoring, support, and enablers once a unit enters service. This requires an ongoing, expert effort per unit for six to 12 months at a minimum. . . .

The Afghan National Army

The fact that there are problems in Afghan force development should not minimize the impact of recent successes. The training effort is far better funded, manned, and structured than it was up to the fall of 2007, and partnering has improved—particularly with the Afghan National Army. The ANA has already proven its value in combat. In the near term, the ANA will play a key role in the shape and clear missions, as well as in the hold mission because the ANP is not yet strong and capable enough to perform the task. The ANA needs to be expanded and fully resourced for its de facto role in the current fight, even while more concerted efforts are made to build an effective ANP for the longer term.

NATO/ISAF and the US must focus in the near term on building up the ANA to carry out critical counterinsurgency tasks and to *hold* in threatened population areas. At the same time, they must improve the ANP and ANCOP [Afghanistan National Civil Order Police] forces so they can provide *hold* capabilities where there is a less serious threat but when, and only when, this is clearly within their current capacity. This effort can only succeed if adequate resources are provided, if adequate time is taken to provide force quality as well as force quantity, and if NATO/ISAF and the US are willing to support the resulting force not only during critical periods of combat, but in phasing it down to a post conflict size that the GIRoA [Government of the Islamic Republic of Afghanistan] can fund and sustain.

CSTC-A [Combined Security Transition Command-Afghanistan, an effort by the United States to assist the Afghan government in training ANSF] has already begun active efforts to expand ANA forces from an assigned strength of roughly 91,000 to 134,000, and from 117 fielded kandaks [battalions] to 179. It is procuring improved equipment and raising the number of commando kandaks from 6 to 8. A total of 76 of the 117 fielded units are already capable of leading operations.

A successful US strategy to win the war in Afghanistan—and to create a true host country partner—does, however, require the full—*and ruthlessly self-honest and objective*—implementation of three additional decisions about the future of the ANA.

1. The first decision is to accelerate training and current force expansion goals, and to set a new goal for expansion of the ANA that will increase it from a goal of 134,000 men to 240,000 in 2014. This will mean a major expansion in funding, in training facilities and trainers, in equipment, and in mentors or partner units. Resources to do this well should be identified and committed concurrently. . . .

2. The second decision is to end the shortfall in NATO and ETT [Embedded Training Team] mentors and resources. . . .

3. The third decision is to create a full operational partnership, focused around the development of the ANA and key elements of the ANP, so that Afghans are a true partner in all NATO/ANSF and US operations and take the lead in joint operations as soon as possible. It is not enough for NATO/ISAF units to partner with the ANSF. The ANSF must be made a full partner at the command level as well. Afghans should see Afghans taking the lead in the field as soon as practical, and as playing a critical role in shaping all plans and operations as well as in implementing *hold and build*. . . .

There is a fourth critical decision that the US, NATO/ISAF, the Afghan government, and the Afghan Ministry of Defense need to make. It is all very well to use a slogan like "shape, clear, hold, and build" [a strategy of removing insurgent elements from populations through both military efforts and outreach to local groups through aid and contact]. It is quite another to systematically implement it as part of a population-centric strategy. No matter how much effort is made to improve the integrity, size, and capability of the various elements of the Afghan police, improve governance at the local level, and create an effective structure for prompt justice—there will be three to five years in which the ANA must play a critical role in various clear and hold efforts, and in solving build problems with local, aid, and government workers. No effort to make a population-centric strategy work—or that relies on hope and rhetoric to make "shape, clear, hold, and build" work without explicit plans that reflect this reality can succeed.

> *"Experts say realizing the new Obama endgame—turning over 'security responsibilities to the Afghans'—will take time, money, and far more resources than have been committed."*

Afghan Security Forces Will Not Soon Be Ready to Take over Military Responsibilities

Greg Bruno

Greg Bruno is a staff writer at the Council on Foreign Relations. In the following viewpoint, he argues that the Afghan National Army and the Afghan National Police forces are understaffed and undertrained and face other significant hurdles. Thus, despite the hopes of foreign governments, including the United States, he concludes that Afghan forces are not likely to be ready to take over security in Afghanistan in the near future.

As you read, consider the following questions:

1. According to Bruno, what was the size of the Afghan army in March 2009?

2. What does Bruno identify as the Afghan army's primary tactical vehicle?

3. According to the author, what will be the police-to-civilian ratio in Afghanistan, and how does this compare to recommended ratios?

In outlining his new strategy [as of April 2009] for the beleaguered Afghan military campaign, U.S. President Barack Obama put Afghanistan's nascent security forces front and center in the U.S. effort to right the mission. Obama announced the deployment of about four thousand additional U.S. troops to train Afghan soldiers which, the president said, will "fully resource our effort to train and support the Afghan army and police" for the first time. Senior U.S. military officials, meanwhile, have said America's exit strategy is tied to Afghanistan's ability to provide its own security, and NATO [North Atlantic Treaty Organization] and coalition partners have embraced the concept that improving the capability of Afghan forces is the quickest way to exit. Japan, for instance, announced plans in February 2009 to pay the salaries of roughly eighty thousand Afghan police officers for six months. And NATO nations in late March 2009 pledged to add upwards of five thousand temporary troops to improve security for elections, as well as to help in training efforts. Yet some analysts warn that building Afghanistan's security apparatus will take more than pledges and cash. Even the top military commander in Afghanistan, Army General David [D.] McKiernan, acknowledges the handover of security to indigenous forces is "years away."

Afghanistan's National Security Forces consist of three principal components—the army, the army air corps, and the national police. Within these units, specialized personnel round out the country's security capabilities, including communications and logistical staff, border guards, and narcotics officers. Yet as sound as the country's security apparatus appears on paper, its effectiveness, professionalism, and state of readiness remain uneven. In March 2009, with violence in Afghanistan at an all-time high, President Obama vowed to "accelerate our efforts to build an Afghan army of 134,000 and a police force of 82,000 so that we can meet these goals by 2011." The U.S. government has spent at least $16.5 billion to train and equip Afghan army and police forces. But experts say realizing the new Obama endgame—turning over "security responsibility to the Afghans"—will take time, money, and far more resources than have been committed.

A breakdown of each security component, and its current state of effectiveness, follows:

The Afghan National Army

The Afghan National Army is widely seen as the most capable branch of the country's security forces. It recruits soldiers nationally, and pays them roughly $100 per month. In March 2009 the Pentagon measured the size of the Afghan army at nearly 83,000, though only 52,000 were engaged in combat alongside international or U.S. forces (an additional 5,400 troops were believed to be AWOL [absent without leave]). This represented full fielding for 95 of a planned 160 units. Structurally, the army is divided into five ground maneuver corps consisting of two to four brigades. Each brigade is comprised of infantry kandaks (Afghan battalions), combat support kandaks, and combat service support kandaks. Once it is expanded to 134,000 soldiers, the army will consist of five corps headquarters, a division headquarters, 21 brigades, and 114 battalions. Since August 2008 the army has assumed lead responsibility for security in Kabul and is extending its reach into some provinces.

Progress notwithstanding, the size of the Afghan force is a point of major contention for U.S., Afghan, and NATO allies. In March 2009 President Obama called for an expansion of the Afghan army to 134,000—a figure that is to include 12,000 trainees—as early as December 2011. But these benchmarks were originally approved by the U.S. military in late 2008, leaving some Afghan officials to question the U.S. president's March 2009 commitment. While the president left open the possibility of "additional enlargements as circumstances and resources warrant," officials closest to the U.S.-led training effort say they were expecting a greatly expanded force—somewhere in the combined 400,000 ballpark. Major Gen. Richard P. Formica, head of the U.S. unit responsible for training Afghan forces, acknowledged in a press call to reporters that his unit had considered "nearly doubling" the size of the Afghan army, a plan some U.S. lawmakers, including Senator Joe Lieberman (I-CT), advocate. Afghan Defense Minister Gen. Abdul Rahim Wardak, meanwhile, told CFR.org [the Council on Foreign Relations Web site] in April 2009 he was under the impression President Obama was set to run with the doubling recommendation, but appears to have changed course without explanation. The final number, Gen. Wardak says, "was a big surprise."

Yet regardless of the Afghan army's long-term growth plans, oversight and sustainability issues continue to plague the force in the near term. A February 2009 analysis by the U.S. Government Accountability Office found that roughly 17 percent of the small arms, mortars, and grenade launchers supplied to the Afghan security services since 2002 are unaccounted for. Meanwhile, the equipment the Afghan army does possess remains a limiting factor, military officials say. Currently, the army's primary tactical vehicle is a Ford Ranger truck, which Gen. Wardak argues provides little in the way of protected mobility. "A small mine hits them and they are gone," he says. Coalition trainers are in the process of augmenting the Afghan forces with up-armored Humvees [military transports], but the conversion will not be completed until mid-2010. Wardak says he has consistently asked U.S. and NATO allies for other material—artillery, rockets, mortars—

but supplies have been slow to materialize. "I was much [better] equipped when we were fighting the Soviets," the Afghan general says.

The army's ability to operate independently has been delayed by these limitations, U.S. military officials acknowledge. As of November 2008 just seven battalions were capable of operating without international support, Pentagon statistics show. This pace is expected to quicken as U.S. and international trainers surge into the country. But even a rapid expansion of the Afghan army will not necessarily bring U.S. involvement to an end. As CFR defense expert Stephen Biddle cautions, building an Afghan army capable of beating back the Taliban [radical Islamist organization leading the insurgency] will cost billions of dollars a year in support, money and time that could prove politically "much more problematic" for American strategists.

The Afghan National Police

Afghanistan's national police are another story. On paper the police force looks solid, with the Afghan Uniform Police responsible for general enforcement and public safety; the [Afghan] Border Police patrolling the country's borders and conducting countersmuggling operations; the [Afghan National] Civil Order Police [responsible] for disturbances in urban areas; the Counter Narcotics Police [of Afghanistan] countering drug trafficking; the Criminal Investigation police investigating crimes; and the counterterrorism police heading counterinsurgency operations. But the Pentagon says development of Afghanistan's police force "has been hindered by lack of institutional reform, widespread corruption, insufficient U.S. military trainers and advisors, and a lack of unity of effort within the international community."

As of November 2008 there were 76,000 police officers; President Obama's plan adds just 6,000 more. Military strategists estimate the proper ratio of police to people in peacetime is around 1 per 400 citizens, while stability operations

Corruption in the Afghan Police Force

The efforts of many honest and effective Afghan police should not be ignored, and one cannot overstate the bravery of those who choose policing in an environment of acute and ever-present danger. Nevertheless, the ANP [Afghan National Police] as a collective is riddled with problems starting with illiteracy, levels of which are currently estimated at 65 percent of the male population. This fundamental problem restricts the quality of recruits, the effectiveness of police training, and even their ability to write reports and record critical information.

It is little wonder, then, that the ANP is regularly deemed ineffective, a problem exacerbated by its members' role as quasi-soldiers rather than civilian police officers. The ANP has the immense challenge of switching between policing duties and supporting full-scale military operations with very little notice. Conversely, too much police time is wasted on non-core duties such as road construction and maintenance. This may be why the public complains that the police are lazy and remiss in their duties, with calls to the emergency 119 number often going unanswered. This conduct is undoubtedly compounded by narcotic use; British officials estimate that 60 percent of the ANP in Helmand [a southwest province] use drugs.

More serious than charges of unprofessionalism, however, the ANP are never far from accusations that they habitually abuse their power. . . .

Andrew Legon, "Ineffective, Unprofessional, and Corrupt: The Afghan National Police Challenge," Foreign Policy Research Institute, June 2009. www.fpri.org.

call for much high ratios. Afghanistan, with an estimated population of 33 million, will have a ratio of 1 to 402 police once the force is fully staffed.

But beyond size, there are serious problems with lack of professionalism. An August 2007 report by the International Crisis Group found that the national police force's misuse of power is so pervasive that "Afghanistan's citizens often view the police more as a source of fear than of security." A follow-on report in December 2008 found little had changed. While international commitments to improving the police's capabilities increased, corruption within Afghan ministries hampered progress. Attrition also remains a problem, as does a lack of effective training and equipment. Even more troubling, the International Crisis Group contends, are efforts by the Taliban to target police officers. In the crosshairs of militants, the death rate for police is now three times higher than soldiers in the Afghan army.

There are signs of progress. For one, the number of units considered "capable of operating independently" by the U.S. military is rising, Pentagon data show. Training initiatives led by the U.S. military—like the so-called Focused District Development program—have brought personnel to Kabul [Afghanistan's capital] for advanced mentoring with international law enforcement experts; future training efforts will focus on countering improvised explosive devices (IEDs), communications upgrades, intelligence advances, and enhanced border surveillance. Gen. Wardak says Afghan officials have also implemented changes to improve police professionalism, such as restricting officers from serving in their home districts to reduce the risk of favoritism to immediate family, extended family, or "the big shot tribal guy."

Other Afghan Security Forces

Afghan National Army Air Corps (ANAAC). The Afghan air corps remains in its infancy. As of late 2008 the Afghan air corps operated and maintained just seven medium cargo planes and a mere thirteen helicopters, though plans were in the works to assign Afghan commando battalions with helicopter detachments for rapid-response missions. Pentagon trainers say the ANAAC will eventually include "reconnaissance and light attack air-to-ground fixed-wing aircraft," but implementation is years off. A 2009 summary of international activities in Afghanistan by NATO reported that the air corps aims to employ 7,000 personnel and 126 aircraft by 2016.

Afghan Public Protection Force. Perhaps the most closely watched, though least understood, element of Afghanistan's security forces is the tribal protection force, an experimental militia program modeled after a successful program in Iraq. President Obama has vowed to "support" this local initiative, which some observers liken to a neighborhood watch. Gen. Wardak says these units are being recruited, and vetted, by regional leaders, who in turn will assume responsibility for their performance and discipline. But some experts of Afghanistan's tribal structure, like Thomas [H.] Johnson of the Naval Postgraduate School, warn that arming local tribes could awaken deep-rooted tribal blood feuds and do more harm than good. . . .

President Obama has pinned high hopes on Afghanistan's security forces, and is committing additional U.S. troops to improving their lot. As many as four thousand additional U.S. military trainers are expected to deploy to Afghanistan in coming months, and coalition partners have said they, too, will bolster mentoring efforts. Allies agreed at the April 2009 NATO summit in France to send an additional three hundred paramilitary trainers and mentors, and a newly dedicated command—NATO Training Mission-Afghanistan—will coordinate the mentoring mission.

Success Will Be Difficult

The additions, long overdue, come at a crucial time. The U.S. military provides the bulk of the training to Afghanistan's security forces, coordinated by the Combined Security Transition Command-Afghanistan and funded by Congress through the Afghan Security Forces Fund. But a November 2008 assessment by the Pentagon found there were only 1,100 embed trainers available for deployment, just half of the military's requirement. NATO training teams have also been in historically short supply. NATO's 2009 assessment of allied efforts in the war noted that by December 2010, the security bloc will require up [to] eighty-two training teams, nearly double the current allotment. That could mean an extra 1,600 NATO forces would be needed at a time when the Obama administration has had difficulty convincing allied forces to send more than a token few.

But even more pragmatic challenges than international trainers loom. For one, analysts say police and soldiers are paid more to fight for the Taliban—$100 per month from the Afghan government, versus $300 a month from the Taliban—a calculus that must be reversed. Coordination among allied efforts is another concern. The International Crisis Group's 2008 report says there remains a need for "enhanced coordination in the efforts of different countries involved in reform, with a greater emphasis on developing Afghan institutions rather than parallel programs." While training efforts are currently divided between U.S., NATO, and EU [European Union] forces, observers say the mission suffers from resource deficiencies and competing agendas. Seth G. Jones and C. Christine Fair of the RAND Corporation noted in a January 2009 study that more than two dozen countries and multilateral organizations contribute "in some measure" to police training. But so far, Jones and Fair write, "results have been disappointing."

Finally, basic operational limitations are increasingly undermining army and police progress. Even today, seven years into the U.S.-led war effort, NATO, U.S., and Afghan forces don't always coordinate their missions, military experts say, and it's not uncommon for U.S. and Afghan forces operating jointly to have no idea what NATO's ISAF [International Security Assistance Force] forces are doing and vice versa. One former senior U.S. military commander in Afghanistan, speaking in a not-for-attribution forum near Washington in early 2009, called "unity of effort" the most serious problem we have in Afghanistan today. "It's not the Taliban. It's not governance. It's not security," he said. "It's the utter failure in the unity of effort department."

Periodical Bibliography

The following articles have been selected to supplement the diverse views presented in this chapter.

Baltimore Sun	"We Must Send More than Troops to Afghanistan," December 22, 2009.
Peter Bergen	"Hardly Winning," *Foreign Policy*, August 11, 2009.
Richard A. Clarke and Steven Simon	"More Troops to Afghanistan?" *Huffington Post*, September 11, 2009.
Gilles Dorronsoro	"The Taliban's Winning Strategy in Afghanistan," Carnegie Endowment for International Peace, June 2009.
James M. Dubik	"Accelerating Combat Power in Afghanistan," Institute for the Study of War, December 2009.
Thomas H. Johnson and M. Chris Mason	"All Counterinsurgency Is Local," *Atlantic*, October 2008.
Robert Maginnis	"Throwing Afghan Security Forces Under the Bus," *Human Events*, December 7, 2009. www.humanevents.com.
Soraya Sarhaddi Nelson	"For U.S., Vast Challenge to Expand Afghan Forces," NPR (National Public Radio), December 22, 2009. www.npr.org.
Eric Schmitt	"Military Faces Challenges in Deploying More Troops to Afghanistan," *New York Times*, December 14, 2009.
Eric Schmitt	"Obama Issues Order for More Troops in Afghanisan," *New York Times*, November 30, 2009.
Abubakar Siddique	"Expansion of Afghan Security Forces Fraught with Challenges," Radio Free Europe/Radio Liberty, March 25, 2009. www.rferl.org.

CHAPTER 2

What Is the Status of Human Rights in Afghanistan?

Chapter Preface

A fghanistan has been at war since the U.S. invasion in 2001. Before that, the country had known only a scant five years of stability, preceded by fifteen years of war. Altogether, that means Afghanistan has been the scene of conflict, with only brief respites, for around three decades. According to a November 18, 2009, nongovernmental organization (NGO) report quoted on the Integrated Regional Information Networks (IRIN), "A whole generation has grown up never having experienced peace, and many Afghans are struggling to cope with the psychological, economic, social and physical ramifications of the conflict, past and present."

In large part, as a result of this constant warfare, Afghanistan is one of the poorest and most troubled countries on earth. An August 14, 2009, BBC News article noted that "Afghanistan has some of the world's worst health indicators." Average life expectancy is forty-four; one in five children die before they are five years old. Maternal care is largely unavailable for rural women, and as a result, one in fifty women die during childbirth. According to David Koch writing in a March 12, 2009, article on the UNICEF (United Nations Children's Fund) Web site, "less than a quarter of all Afghans" have access to safe water supplies.

Disease is a serious problem in Afghanistan as well. According to the 2009 U.S. Agency for International Development (USAID) infectious diseases report on Afghanistan, "46,000 new TB [tuberculosis] cases occur annually in Afghanistan," with women infected twice as often as men. Typhoid, malaria, and polio are also common in Afghanistan, as are diseases caused by contaminated food and water. HIV/AIDS is also a growing problem, though the exact level of the problem is difficult to determine since the disease "remains almost completely underground, shrouded in ignorance and stigma," according to Carlotta Gall writing in a *New York Times* article on March 18, 2007.

Like health care, education in Afghanistan is inadequate. Under Taliban rule, Afghan women were forbidden to attend school. Things have "greatly improved," since then, according to Abdullah Qazi writing in an April 10, 2008, article on the Web site Afghanistan Online. Qazi noted that more than 5.4 million Afghan children attend school, and that 35 percent of them are girls, with the result that "more Afghans now attend school or receive some sort of education than ever in its modern history." Despite such gains, however, 63 percent of men and 90 percent of women in rural areas are illiterate, according to a May 22, 2009, article on ReliefWeb.

The viewpoints in this chapter examine other areas in which Afghanistan faces challenges in protecting human welfare and human rights.

"At the moment, U.S. and NATO forces seem unable or unwilling to adopt tactics less lethal to the civilian population."

The United States Makes Little Effort to Prevent Civilian Casualties in Afghanistan

Eliza Szabo

Eliza Szabo is a research associate at the Center for Defense Information. In the following viewpoint, she argues that the United States and its allies have done little to prevent civilian deaths in Afghanistan. She also notes that numbers of civilian deaths in Afghanistan are difficult to determine because the problem has been largely ignored. She concludes that the issue is becoming a higher priority, and she hopes that better figures and, more importantly, fewer civilian deaths may result.

As you read, consider the following questions:

1. According to an ISAF spokeswoman, why has air power been so important to the military effort in Afghanistan?

2. How many civilians does Amnesty International estimate were killed in Afghanistan in 2006?

3. According to Szabo, what kind of figures on civilian deaths are maintained by the U.S. Department of Defense and the British Ministry of Defence?

Almost six years ago [in 2001], U.S. and allied forces toppled the [extreme Islamist] Taliban regime in Afghanistan, paving the way for a pro-Western, interim government and the country's first post-Taliban presidential elections. Throughout the war, however, there has been little focus—whether from government or watchdog groups—on its toll on the civilian population of Afghanistan.

No Data for Civilian Deaths

Very few attempts at compiling annual estimates of insurgency-related civilian deaths have been made. The nature of the conflict makes data collection difficult and verification even more so. Figures are often at least partially based on secondary information—such as reports issued by government officials, the media, or other organizations working in Afghanistan—which can be difficult to corroborate. Consequently, the number of civilian deaths in Afghanistan is uncertain, despite the recent proliferation of estimates.

According to what little information is available, U.S. and NATO-led [North Atlantic Treaty Organization–led] forces appear to be responsible for a growing number of civilian deaths. Despite its reluctance to quantify the situation, the UN [United Nations] publicly reported on June 2, 2007, that its data indicates "the number of [civilian] deaths attributed to pro-government forces marginally exceeds that caused by anti-government forces."

U.S. and NATO officials stress that insurgent fighters hide among the civilian population and use them as human shields, but the fact remains that, whatever the causes, this rising civilian death rate undermines the strategic goals of the United States and its allies. The growing perception that Western forces are unconcerned with and a direct threat to the safety of civilians makes the Afghan population less inclined to side with the West against the Taliban [now leading the insurgency]. Also, Afghans will be less likely to support a government seen as aiding or cooperating with Western forces; hence, the recent statements by President Hamid Karzai reprimanding U.S. and NATO forces for their apparent disregard for Afghan civilian life. Tensions over the issue not only threaten the relationship between the Afghan and coalition governments, but among coalition members themselves as they debate an appropriate response to the mounting toll.

At the moment, U.S. and NATO forces seem unable or unwilling to adopt tactics less lethal to the civilian population. Expressions of regret and reiterations of respect by the military sound increasingly empty as U.S and NATO air strikes continue to attack residential buildings believed to contain Taliban insurgents, but that time after time are found to also house civilians. An International Security Assistance Force (ISAF) [the NATO military force in Afghanistan] spokeswoman was recently quoted as saying, "We are looking closely at our air operations, but it would not be something we would be looking to change at this point." She cited the limited number of troops available as a primary reason for maintaining the current role of air power in the conflict.

Death Toll Estimates

The issue has spurred a number of groups and organizations to begin tallying Afghan civilians killed this year [2007]. The British Agencies Afghanistan Group (BAAG) estimated somewhere between 400 and 500 civilians were killed between January and the end of May 2007. The Afghanistan NGO [nongovernmental organization] Safety Office (ANSO) [which coordinates security for relief organizations] reports 452 civilian deaths during the same time period, 189 of which were caused by U.S. and NATO forces. As of June 23, the Associated

Press [AP] counted 381 civilian deaths in 2007, 203 of which resulted from U.S. and NATO operations. The Agency Coordinating Body for Afghan Relief reported that progovernment forces were responsible for 230 civilian deaths in 2007. On July 3, the UN Office for the Coordination of Humanitarian Affairs reported Afghanistan Independent Human Rights Commission figures for 2007: Over 270 civilian deaths [were] caused by international military operations out of a total of at least 540. A July 1 AP report cited a UN count of 593 total civilian deaths in 2007, 314 of which were caused by international or Afghan military action. The highest number of civilians killed in U.S. and NATO operations this year was reported by Dr. Marc Herold of the University of New Hampshire, who estimated somewhere between 388 and 523 deaths between Jan. 1 and June 22, 2007.

Research revealed only two estimates of civilian deaths in the first three months of the war. Herold's online database counts Afghan civilian casualties reported by the media. He estimates 2,567–2,947 civilians were killed in U.S. aerial bombings between Oct. 7 and Dec. 10, 2001. Carl Conetta, codirector of the Project on Defense Alternatives, a project that researches security policy and its challenges, estimates anywhere from 1,000 to 1,300 Afghan civilian deaths due to U.S. aerial bombardment between Oct. 7, 2001 and Jan. 10, 2002. Conetta attributes what appears to be a minimum of 3,000 additional civilian deaths to the impact of the conflict on the nation's refugee and famine crises. The Herold and Conetta studies were based exclusively on media reports and are evidently the only attempts that have been made to quantify Afghan civilian deaths during the outbreak of war in 2001.

No annual estimates are currently available for the subsequent years 2002 through 2005, although Human Rights Watch and ANSO are reportedly in the process of back-cataloging information collected prior to 2006. In the organization's January *World Report 2007*, Human Rights Watch asserted that the number of Afghans killed in insurgency-related violence in

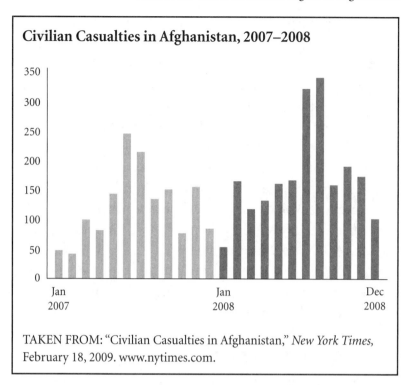

Civilian Casualties in Afghanistan, 2007–2008

TAKEN FROM: "Civilian Casualties in Afghanistan," *New York Times*, February 18, 2009. www.nytimes.com.

2006, estimated in the report as at least 1,000, was "twice as many as in 2005 and more than any other year since the 2001 fall of the Taliban." A more detailed report released in April estimated at least 899 total insurgency-related civilian deaths, but described the figure as conservative. The estimate drew from a wide range of sources—the group's own research and interviews, ANSO reports, media reports, statements by government officials, NGOs, and spokesmen of insurgent groups—and is arguably the most substantiated figure currently available for 2006.

Amnesty International's 2006 estimate of 1,000 insurgency-related civilian deaths was based on information provided in government documents and media reports. A BAAG employee gave an offhand estimate of about 1,000 as well. The International Committee of the Red Cross reported 670 civilian deaths in 2006. The figure is based on information provided by Afghan government officials.

A number of other organizations started keeping track of insurgency-related civilian deaths in 2007. The Associated Press began compiling information collected and reported by staff writers to calculate its own tallies. Also, in a May 28, 2007, press briefing, chief of human rights at the UN Assistance Mission in Afghanistan [UNAMA] Richard Bennett announced the development of a civilian casualties database. He warned, however, that much of the information available is "second- or third-hand" and, thus unverified. UN officials have recently avoided issuing public estimates, emphasizing the difficulties involved in collecting and corroborating information. A UNAMA official explained that UN numbers recently reported by AP were never intended for public release, as they represent only a rough estimate. The real count, he speculated, is likely to be higher.

More Attention Is Needed

NATO's International Security Assistance Force (ISAF) is also tracking civilian deaths, apparently through its medical facilities, but a press officer warned that their numbers "might not be entirely accurate." ISAF does not release estimates to the public. NATO accounts of civilians killed in individual incidents are often inconsistent with estimates from Afghan officials. For example, a NATO spokesman was quoted in a July 2, 2007, *New York Times* article regarding recent air strikes in Helmand province as saying, "we want to make it clear that we at this point believe the numbers [of civilians killed in the incident] are a dozen or less." Afghan officials, however, reported that the strikes resulted in 45 civilian deaths. Elsewhere in the province, barely three days earlier, Afghan officials reported up to 60 civilians killed in fighting and U.S.-led air strikes. A NATO spokesman said that the military could not confirm "numbers that large" and issued an often-used statement about enemy fighters willingly endangering civilian lives.

A U.S. government news release acknowledged that some civilians were killed in the attacks, but did not include an estimated number.

When questioned about whether or not the Department of Defense (DOD) maintains any records of Afghan civilian deaths, a DOD official stated that they maintain documentation on U.S. military personnel only. The British Ministry of Defence replied similarly to an inquiry under the Freedom of Information Act (FOIA) 2000, stating that it "does not maintain records that would enable a definitive number of civilian fatalities to be recorded." Though figures issued by local Afghan officials are often cited in the media, it is unclear whether the Afghan government keeps centralized records of civilian casualties, which would enable it to issue annual estimates.

The difficulties in collecting accurate information on civilian casualties in Afghanistan have been compounded by the fact that only recently has the issue been given the attention it deserves. The first annual estimates that attempt to include all insurgency-related civilian deaths came out in 2007 for the previous year, leaving five years during which the U.S. and Afghan governments, human rights groups and other nongovernmental organizations, and the media did not provide the information to the public. This year's increased efforts to monitor the situation and to review conditions in the past may reflect on the fact that more civilians are becoming casualties of the war; hopefully, this also shows an increased awareness of the issue's serious implications for the war's ultimate outcome.

The failure of those supporting the Karzai government—particularly the U.S. government and NATO—to collect or make information on the issue public suggests a refusal to acknowledge the negative impacts this war is having on Afghanistan, and perhaps, the grave direction it's headed.

> *"Even the most comprehensive safe-guards can fail under the stress and confusion of combat against an enemy that ... often uses civilians as human shields."*

It Is Difficult for the United States to Limit Civilian Casualties in Afghanistan

David Zucchino

David Zucchino is a Los Angeles Times *reporter and the author of* Thunder Run: The Armored Strike to Capture Baghdad. *In the following viewpoint, he argues that the United States is com-mitted to reducing civilian casualties but that doing so is very difficult given the conditions in Afghanistan. He notes that air strikes are essential in the battle against the Taliban. He adds that mistakes are very difficult to prevent in high-stress, life-and-death combat situations.*

As you read, consider the following questions:

1. According to General Stanley A. McChrystal, what should the measure of success be in Afghanistan?

2. According to Afghan officials, how many civilians were killed in the May 4, 2009, incident? How many were killed according to U.S. estimates?

3. According to Zucchino, most deaths from air strikes occur during what kind of mission?

When Afghan parliament member Obaidullah Helali went to visit his constituents in the village of Garani last month, they confronted him with clubs and stones.

It was three days after a U.S. air strike killed dozens of civilians in the remote settlement in the western province of Farah. Enraged villagers threatened to beat Helali and other officials and asked why the Afghan government couldn't protect them—not from the Taliban, but from the U.S. military.

"If the Americans don't stop these kind of accidents, the people will never believe the government will keep them safe," Helali said.

But experiences such as the fateful May 4 air strike show that halting civilian deaths will not be easy. Fighter pilots and air controllers at the main U.S. air base here, near Kabul, the Afghan capital, say that even the most comprehensive safeguards can fail under the stress and confusion of combat against an enemy that they say often uses civilians as human shields.

The mounting death toll of Afghan civilians from U.S. air strikes has unleashed a tide of resentment and fury that threatens to undermine the American counterinsurgency effort. From President Obama to the new U.S. commander in Afghanistan, Army Gen. Stanley A. McChrystal, American officials have made the reduction of civilian deaths a top priority as they revamp their strategy.

McChrystal, who took command this week, told Congress that the measure of success in Afghanistan should be the number of civilians protected, not the number of insurgents killed. Reducing civilian casualties is "essential to our credibility," he said.

The U.S. military employs a lengthy set of precautions, including written rules of engagement and multiple levels of approval before bombs can be dropped or missiles launched.

To gauge each mission's risk to civilians, a collateral damage estimate, or CDE, is prepared.

Yet civilian deaths continue to mount. U.S. commanders have not specified how they intend to reduce them, except to continue rigorously reviewing and enforcing existing restrictions. But the nature of the war almost guarantees more accidental deaths.

When people make split-second life-or-death decisions, and face what they consider a choice between protecting their compatriots or civilians, the decisions have proved imperfect.

"We have a very smart enemy who understands our weakness," said Air Force Col. Steven Kwast, an F-15 pilot who commands the 455th Air Expeditionary Wing at Bagram.

"And our weakness is the fact that this counterinsurgency is not about killing the enemy," he said. "It's about protecting the civilians of Afghanistan. . . . The enemy is good about drawing us into a dilemma we can't get out of without losing coalition lives."

A preliminary Pentagon investigation of the May 4 incident—the final report is expected within days—found that mistakes were made in the fighting that led to the air strikes.

U.S. Marines called in Air Force and Navy warplanes after the Afghan army and police were attacked by insurgents. One aircraft was cleared to drop bombs but the pilot briefly lost sight of the target while circling to get into position to attack, the preliminary investigative report says. It also questions whether a B-1 bomber strike on a village compound was necessary at one point in the 8 1/2-hour battle when Afghan forces were not under direct attack.

"In a perfect world, that pilot would have never lost sight, even for a few seconds, of those combatants shooting at our friendlies" and possibly mingling with civilians, Kwast said. "But you have to take the criticism and say, hey, we could have done better."

Marines called in the air strikes after Afghan army and police forces they were mentoring ignored warnings and went to root out insurgents in the village, where they were ambushed, an American security specialist said in Kabul.

Neither U.S. nor Afghan forces secured the village until two days after the attack, allowing the Taliban to control the area and information about the attack, the security specialist said.

The specialist, who has visited the attack site, said insurgent movements reported by Marines late in the battle might also have included civilians running for cover.

After the attack, the specialist said, the U.S. and Afghan governments made solatia, or condolence, payments. They apologized. And they held a council meeting two weeks later that included Afghan President Hamid Karzai and top U.S. diplomats.

Helali and other Afghan officials say 140 civilians were killed. The U.S. estimates that 26 died.

Abdul Ghafar Watandar, the police chief in Farah province, said in an interview that the final death toll could be 75 to 78. He said some villagers could not come up with confirmed names of family members they claimed were killed. He suspected they were fraudulently seeking condolence payments.

Qari Yousef Ahmadi, a Taliban spokesman, claimed in a telephone interview that U.S. forces target civilians "because they are here to kill all Afghans," not just insurgents. He denied that Taliban fighters mingled with civilians in the May 4 incident.

More Civilian Deaths

In an incident that could seriously undermine the central U.S. aim in Afghanistan, dozens of civilians were killed or injured early Friday [September 4, 2009] in a NATO [North Atlantic Treaty Organization] air strike, Afghan authorities said.

The predawn strike on a pair of hijacked fuel tankers in a remote part of northern Kunduz province killed more than 70 people, most of them civilians, according to Afghan police, provincial officials and doctors.

Dozens of villagers suffered serious burns in the massive fireball ignited when the tankers were hit, they said.

M. Karim Faiez and Laura King,
"Civilian Deaths Reported After NATO Airstrikes Kill up to
90 in Afghanistan," Los Angeles Times, September 5, 2009.

A recent United Nations report says air strikes accounted for 64% of the 828 civilians killed last year by U.S. or Afghan government forces. About 1,160 civilians died at the hands of the Taliban or other insurgents.

"People are very angry, because these things happen over and over again," Watandar said. "They don't trust the Americans when they say they don't do this on purpose and they have ways to keep it from happening again."

Air Force commanders and pilots say they have not been given new procedures as a result of the renewed focus on civilian deaths. But they have received a clear message that finding ways to reduce such mistakes is paramount, particularly because the Taliban uses such incidents for propaganda purposes.

"There are additional changes that I think we're going to clearly have to make to ensure that we do absolutely everything to make sure civilian casualties are eliminated, if possible, or certainly minimized in every situation," Adm. Michael G. Mullen, chairman of the Joint Chiefs of Staff, said Thursday.

But air supremacy is essential. Without it, thinly stretched ground forces would not have the latitude to pursue the Taliban into remote, rugged areas where they are more prone to be ambushed and cut off.

Insurgents "know air power is something they can't defend," Kwast said. "If they could, they would have the freedom of movement and maneuver to win."

Ground commanders say that before any air strike is authorized, they work with pilots and Air Force controllers to locate friendly forces, civilians and insurgents. At the same time, commanders back at bases talk to them by radio while watching video feeds from satellites or drones.

When an air strike is approved, the ground controller can give pilots a "nine-line," a detailed set of instructions that includes target coordinates, the type of weapon to be used, the angle of attack and any restrictions.

The ground commander is in charge, but Air Force controllers and pilots may refuse to fire if they believe rules of engagement might be violated. They may also abort if they see a sudden change, such as insurgents darting into a home.

Only the controller, not the ground commander, can tell the pilot that he is "cleared hot," or cleared to fire.

"We own those weapons when they come off the airplane," said Capt. Ryan McLean, 31, an A-10 Warthog pilot. "If something goes wrong with that weapon, then we are held accountable, even if that ground commander was on the radio screaming for it."

Capt. Terry Gable, 28, who flies an F-15, said pilots are trained to avoid using their weapons if possible. They make low passes or launch nonlethal targeting rockets to try to force insurgents to stop firing. The intent is to avoid accidental killings of civilians or friendly forces.

"It's not all about dropping bombs or shooting the weapons," Gable said. "We go through multiple checklists to make sure the ground guys and us have done everything to make sure buildings are cleared of civilians. And only as a last resort are we going to go kinetic [fire weapons] in order to end contact."

So-called preplanned air missions are carefully vetted in advance, but the decision-making speeds up when fighter pilots are suddenly called in to support troops under fire. The majority of civilian deaths from air strikes come during such "troops in contact" missions, when pilots, controllers and commanders are faced with rapidly changing conditions and life-or-death decisions.

"Human beings under great stress, under the fear of death, make mistakes," Col. Kwast said. "If you do not do this perfectly, you will kill a lot of coalition forces. They'll be forced to take risks and die because they were not allowed to defend themselves. That's exactly what the enemy wants."

Pilots say the issue is not the procedures, but making sure that they are followed scrupulously. They say that after each mission, they spend several hours discussing every detail that went right or wrong, probing for errors. Internal procedures are refined constantly.

Kwast said adhering to procedures every second of every mission is crucial.

"The trick is to have processes and procedures so rigorous and so defined that you minimize mistakes without tipping the balance so that you kill more Americans," he said.

"That is the million-dollar question. And we deal with that every mission."

> *"Women are civil society. We've learned all over the world that the only way to develop a stable society and economy is with the education and inclusion of women."*

The United States Must Stay in Afghanistan to Fight for Women's Rights

Ellen Goodman

Ellen Goodman is a Pulitzer Prize–winning columnist for the Boston Globe. In the following viewpoint, she argues that the gains Afghan women experienced after the 2001 U.S. invasion of the country have been squandered for political reasons. She believes that the United States should not abandon Afghan women, but should instead try to rebuild civil society in Afghanistan by including females.

As you read, consider the following questions:

1. According to Goodman, what was the greatest human rights disaster for women in history?

Ellen Goodman, "Afghanistan's Forgotten Class," *The Boston Globe*, November 6, 2009. Copyright © 2009 Globe Newspaper Company. Reproduced by permission of the author.

2. Which Afghan women's group is for, and which is against, the withdrawal of U.S. troops?

3. According to Goodman, what fraction of Afghan students are girls?

It's been 11 years since I looked through a photo album smuggled out of Afghanistan by a brave young woman. "This is a doctor," she said, pointing to one picture. "This is a teacher." It was impossible to tell one woman from another under the burqas enforced by their Taliban rulers.

Back then, the world had turned a cataract eye on Afghan women. Under virtual house arrest, they were forbidden from work, from school, from walking alone or even laughing out loud. It was arguably the greatest human rights disaster for women in history.

After 9/11, when we went after al Qaeda and the Taliban who had hosted these terrorists, many saw collateral virtue in the liberation of Afghan women. Indeed, President Bush played this moral card in his 2002 State of the Union speech when he declared to thunderous applause: "Today women are free, and are part of Afghanistan's new government." Mission accomplished.

Many women shed their burqas, opened schools, entered Parliament. Equal rights were written into the constitution. But slowly, as America turned to the disastrous misadventure in Iraq, Afghan women's freedoms were casually traded in like chits for power.

Now again, we're focusing on this beleaguered country and its sham leader. The discussion is cast in military terms— more troops, less troops. Yet I keep thinking about the women who are once again pushed to the outskirts of the conversation, as if they were an add-on rather than a central factor.

Have you heard this old proverb? Whether the rock hits the pitcher or the pitcher hits the rock, it's going to be bad for the pitcher. Women are the pitcher in this story.

If we abandon the country, or even the countryside, don't we abandon those girls who have gone to school even when risking acid thrown in their eyes? If we prop up the deeply corrupt government of President Hamid Karzai, are we just supporting warlord fundamentalists instead of Taliban fundamentalists?

The options are so chilling that even Afghan women's groups are divided. RAWA, the Revolutionary Association of the Women of Afghanistan, wants us out. WAW, the Women for Afghan Women, "deeply regrets having a position in favor of maintaining, even increasing troops" rather than "abandoning 15 million women and children to madmen."

American women seem equally torn—ambivalent is far too gentle a word. The Feminist Majority Foundation, which championed Afghan women long before it was popular, has stopped short of asking for more troops. Ellie Smeal's anger at American funding of warlords is matched by the fear that if we back out, it will create "terrible human suffering," the return of the prison state. Ann Jones, author of *Kabul in Winter*, confesses to agonizing about deserting Afghan women while fearing that Karzai's henchmen and the Taliban are "brothers under the skin." And Susannah Sirkin of Physicians for Human Rights says ruefully, "I don't think if you ask women and girls that they would easily say their lives are better since 2001. The best you could say is that there is more cause for hope."

We shouldn't be surprised we have come to this pass. It happened on our watch. We barely noticed when Karzai signed a law that would have, among other things, allowed Shi'ite men to withhold food from wives who refused sex. It didn't take a rigged election to show a shallow respect for democracy. If by democracy, that is, you include half the population that is female.

Today, one-third of Afghan students are girls. Women now get health care once denied them. Is that enough? How much

Fragile Gains for Afghan Women

The diminishing status of women's rights in Afghanistan came back into focus in March 2009 when the Shia Personal Status Law, which was riddled with Taliban-style misogyny, was passed by parliament and signed by President Hamid Karzai. The law regulates the personal affairs of Shia Muslims, including divorce, inheritance, and minimum age of marriage, but ... severely restricts women's basic freedoms....

Afghan women's rights activists were galvanized and mounted a successful campaign to force the president to revise the law, aided by the outspokenness of countries like the US, Canada, and various European nations. Unfortunately, the final outcome fell far short of expectations, apparently because President Karzai was intent on maintaining the electoral support of Shia fundamentalists. A month before the presidential election, he issued by decree an amended version of the law which still includes articles that impose drastic restrictions upon Shia women, including the requirement that wives seek their husbands' permission before leaving home except for unspecified "reasonable legal reasons." The law also gives child custody rights to fathers and grandfathers, not mothers or grandmothers, and allows a husband to cease maintenance to his wife if she does not meet her marital duties, including sexual duties.

The furor over the Shia law highlighted the fragility of the gains made by Afghan women, human rights activists, and reform-minded politicians.

Human Rights Watch,
We Have the Promises of the World,
December 6, 2009. www.hrw.org.

are we willing to pay in lives and treasure for hope? How much are we willing to lose in moral suasion, in our own eyes and those of the world, if we abandon these women?

I find this a bleak and demoralizing set of choices. The least unbearable may be to protect the population centers while rebuilding Afghan civil society, one city, one school, one health center at a time. But this works only if we include women in a debate that has been as militarized as war itself.

Afghan women are not the "add-on," the incidentals in this process. Women *are* civil society. We've learned all over the world that the only way to develop a stable society and economy is with the education and inclusion of women. There is no democracy without women.

So, here we go. This is our last chance. And theirs.

> *"People wrongly assume that the Taliban is a sort of alien force, imposing misogynistic views on an unwilling society."*

The U.S. Presence in Afghanistan Does Little for Women's Rights

Anand Gopal

Anand Gopal is an Afghanistan-based journalist. In the following viewpoint, he argues that oppression of women is deeply ingrained in Afghan society, especially in rural areas. He contends that U.S. intervention has done little to improve the lives of most women and that U.S. support for misogynist elements in Afghanistan has actually worsened matters. He concludes that the best thing the United States could do is to stop supporting fundamentalists and misogynists in the country.

As you read, consider the following questions:

1. According to Womankind, what percentage of marriages in Afghanistan are forced and what percentage of brides are under sixteen?

2. According to Gopal, what is the Pashtun man honor-bound to defend?

3. Who were the mujahideen, and who supported them during the 1980s, according to Gopal?

Just as the world's eyes are turning towards Afghanistan once again [in April 2009], a few conservative Afghan lawmakers are trying to pass a law that would, amongst other things, legalize marital rape, prohibit women from leaving the home without permission, deny them the right of inheritance, force a woman to "preen for her husband as and when he desires," and set the minimum female marital age to sixteen.

The draft proposal, which is aimed only at the country's Shia [Muslim] minority, recalls for many the harsh strictures of the Taliban [the radical Islamic group that ruled Afghanistan from 1996 to 2001] era and has been roundly condemned in the international community: [U.S. Secretary of State] Hillary Clinton said that she is "deeply concerned" about the law, [U.S. President Barack] Obama found it "abhorrent", and others in the West have asked, "Is this what our soldiers are dying for?" The international condemnation has forced the [Afghan President Hamid] Karzai administration to shelve the law for the time being, as the Afghan government pledges to look at the details of the bill more closely.

While the world buzzes about this latest setback for Afghan women, you might be wondering just what exactly the bill says about women's rights in Afghanistan.

What Do Afghan Women Think About This Law?

Most Afghan women have never heard of it. This is because the majority of Afghans are rural, living without electricity or a connection to the happenings in Kabul [the capital]. Afghan women suffer from the lowest literacy rate in the world, at 13 percent. And the ones that are familiar with it mostly shrug their shoulders, because the conditions that the law imposes are no different than those that already exist in their everyday lives. The typical woman from the country's south or east, for example, cannot leave her home without a male guardian. She must wear the *burqa* [an outer garment that covers the entire body] in public at all times, and in some villages she must even don one in private. Marital rape is the norm in a society where sex is a man's right, not a woman's.

According to the UK-based [United Kingdom-based] NGO [nongovernmental organization] Womankind [Worldwide], anywhere between 60 and 80 percent of marriages are forced, 57 percent of brides are under the age of 16, and 87 percent complain of domestic violence. UNIFEM [United Nations Development Fund for Women] says that 65 percent of widows in Kabul see suicide as their only option to "get rid of their miseries and desolation." Thousands of women turn to self-immolation every year. There are no reliable stats on rape, as most women will never report it. This is because women can be convicted of *zina*, extramarital sex, if knowledge of the rape becomes public. In most of the country, even a woman just found outside of her home without the permission of her male guardian will be thrown in jail and tried as an adulterer.

How Do Afghan Women Fare Now Compared to the Taliban Era?

The answer [of women's status since 2001], like most things in Afghanistan, depends on where you look and whom you ask. In the central highlands, for example, women of the ethnic minority group the Hazaras are usually allowed to leave the home and sometimes even find work. In Kabul, some females now have access to education, and there are well-paying NGO jobs available for the elite. Only 5 percent of girls go to secondary school throughout the country, but in Kabul more girls are enrolled than at any point in the last ten years.

In the south and east, life for women is mostly unchanged since the Taliban times: They remain cloistered indoors, in burqas, away from schools, without health care, without independence, and without protection from physical and sexual violence. And in some ways, life is even worse than during the Taliban: These women now live in an active war zone, caught in a cross fire between belligerents.

So the lives of women in the central highlands and in some cities have improved, while things have remained the same or even gotten worse for women elsewhere. The sum result is that things have mostly stayed the same for Afghan women since the fall of the Taliban. It shouldn't be surprising that the Organisation for Economic Co-operation and Development recently released a study finding that Afghanistan is the second most unequal society in terms of gender in the world. Or that Afghan women rank at or near the bottom in almost every conceivable world ranking: life expectancy, maternal mortality, access to education, access to health care, suicide rates, domestic violence, and more. In short, Afghanistan is just about the worst place in the world to be a woman.

People wrongly assume that the Taliban is a sort of alien force, imposing misogynistic views on an unwilling society. For instance, Ellen Goodman of the Washington Post Writers Group writes in a recent editorial that:

> Afghan women had slowly gained rights through the 20th century. They helped write their country's 1964 constitution. They served in parliament and went to universities. They were 40 percent of the doctors and 70 percent of the teachers. Then the Taliban turned their homeland into a patriarchal jail.

This couldn't be further from the truth. Afghan women did gain rights throughout the twentieth century—in the cities. In the countryside, where the majority lived, no such

The Status of Afghan Women and Girls, 2008

- The estimated literacy rate for women stands at 15.8% (compared to 31% for men).

- Only 19% of schools are designated as girls' schools.

- In 29% of educational districts there are no designated girls' schools at all.

- Only about 28.4% of teachers in Afghanistan were women in 2005.

- At the primary level there is one girl student for every two boys.

- At the secondary level there is one girl for every three to four boys.

- The number of girls in secondary school decreased by 4.7% per annum during 2004–5.

UNIFEM Afghanistan,
"Afghan Women Fact Sheet 2008."
http://afghanistan.unifem.org.

thing happened. And the Taliban did not turn the Afghan homeland into a patriarchal jail; it was already a prison for women.

Rural Afghanistan's Patriarchal Foundations

There are three causes for women's predicament. First, Afghanistan was and is a rural society, and in the south and east dominated by tribes. This tribal society is deeply patriarchal, with women commodified into a resource to be bartered, sold and fought over. Hence the Pashtun [an ethnic group from which much of the Taliban's support derives] man is honor-bound to defend *zan, zamin* and *zar* (woman, gold and land).

Various Afghan leaders—including some kings and the Communist government—tried in vain to modernize the countryside. But this was a second reason why women remained oppressed—the central state has been weak and unable to successfully enact reforms throughout the country.

Even as the central state made such attempts, other actors were actively working to undermine women's interests in the country. The third reason for the situation today is foreign intervention, especially by Pakistan, Saudi Arabia and the United States. The US and its allies supported the *mujahideen*—fundamentalist, misogynist warlords—against the Soviets in the eighties. The *mujahideen* transformed an extremely reactionary interpretation of Islam into the national standard, and in many ways were even worse than the Taliban. They burned down schools and libraries, killed women in public positions, enforced the burqa in areas under their control. They raped and killed thousands. After coming to power in the mid-nineties, they established a Ministry for the Promotion of Virtue and Prevention of Vice. One issued decree mandated that:

> Women do not need to leave their homes at all, unless absolutely necessary, in which case they are to cover themselves completely; are not to wear attractive clothing and decorative accessories; do not wear perfume; their jewelry must not make any noise; they are not to walk gracefully or with pride and in the middle of the sidewalk; are not to talk to strangers; are not to speak loudly or laugh in public; and they must always ask their husbands' permission to leave home.

When the Taliban arrived in Kabul in 1996, they continued to enforce these mandates, without resorting to the widespread raping and killing that marked the *mujahideen* government.

After the Taliban was toppled, the US and rest of the international community supported these same *mujahideen* in their return to power. The majority of the Afghan parliament today consists of these warlords. Is it any surprise then that parliament tries to pass anti-women laws?

Can the West Save Afghan Women?

Many observers say that unless the rural, tribal structure of the society is changed, the patriarchal prison will continue. But that might be something only the Afghans themselves can accomplish. In the meantime, many Afghan women say that the West can help this process—by dropping support for fundamentalists and misogynists.

It will be important to take such a step, they say, because the West has a credibility gap—despite billions of dollars, thousands of lives lost, and scores of promises, Western intervention has not made the lives of Afghan women significantly better.

> *"Despite the many challenges facing Afghanistan, the country can boast some major successes and perhaps none is more amazing than the success of its media. In name, at least, we now have a free press."*

Freedom of the Press Is Improving in Afghanistan

Saad Mohseni

Saad Mohseni is a director of the Moby Media Group, which owns and operates numerous Afghan media outlets, including Tolo TV, Lemar TV, Arman FM, *and* Afghan Scene *magazine. In the following viewpoint, Mohseni argues that press freedom in Afghanistan has made great advances. He worries, however, that some of these freedoms will be curtailed, noting government press censorship and intimidation of journalists. Mohseni concludes that Afghan democracy requires press freedom.*

As you read, consider the following questions:

1. What groups does Mohseni say put pressure on Afghan free media?

2. According to Mohseni, do young people in Afghanistan want more or less censorship of music videos?

3. What is RTA and why has it received international funding, according to the author?

Despite the many challenges facing Afghanistan, the country can boast some major successes and perhaps none is more amazing than the success of its media. In name, at least, we now have a free press.

The Media Flourish Despite Pressure

Afghanistan today boasts seven private television channels, dozens of private radio stations and hundreds of newspapers and magazines. Media of all sorts in Afghanistan have flourished and could be used as a model for other Central and South Asian nations moving toward democracy, and this no doubt will shape President Hamid Karzai's legacy in the decades to come.

Over the past year [2006–07], however, there have been troubling signs that not everyone in the Afghan government supports this development. The pressure comes on many fronts.

Some of the heat comes from Islamists who fear that free media will corrupt Afghan morals. Some attempts to constrain the press draw support from corrupt politicians who fear their misdeeds will be exposed by enterprising reporters. Others fear that the media's reporting on war crimes from the past two decades will awaken old demons and create unnecessary social tensions. Some officials are simply uncomfortable with the idea of a free press and are genuinely afraid open media will destabilize the young regime.

These elements exert influence in complex and often opaque ways. As far as we can tell from the outside, the Ministry of Information and Culture is the main center of anti-press activity. Several high-profile incidents, especially a conflict between Minister Abdul Karim Khurram and the management of government-controlled Radio Television Afghanistan, raise questions about Mr. Khurram's commitment to a free press. He has also spearheaded moves to stop the broadcast of programs of Al Jazeera English [an independent Middle East news network] by Lemar TV, asking the Attorney General's Office to press charges against the broadcaster despite the lack of any law authorizing such a prosecution.

As for Mr. Karzai, despite his obvious commitment to democracy, there are signs that he might have so much on his plate that media freedom is slipping through the cracks as he tries to kick-start the economy, clamp down on corruption, eradicate narcotics, and fight terrorists and insurgents. That, at least, is one explanation for his Independence Day address on Aug. 19 [2006], in which, rather than congratulating the free press for its achievements despite horrendous conditions, he chose to criticize the media for exceeding their mandate and urged them to control themselves more.

Unsettling Trends

Presidential speeches aside, the growing pattern of pressure on the media has manifested itself in a variety of more worrying ways over the past 12 months.

The government has sought to impose standards limiting "negative" stories from the battlefield through a curious three-page document bearing the hallmarks of a new regulation that was delivered to the media on June 18, 2006. Among the prohibited activities: "Broadcasting and publication of provocative articles which are against the mujahideen [who fought the Soviets in the 1980s] and call them 'warlords' and those which call technocrats as 'Westernized' and subjects of this nature which create division and conflict." The paper also admonished news outlets, among other things, that "news of terrorist activities must not come as the lead story of the news." The document lacked legal force since it had not been enacted by parliament, and it was quickly withdrawn when a controversy erupted, but the fact that it was prepared in the first place is a troubling sign.

Journalists are also increasingly subject to arrest and detention without charge. The most recent example is the detention on Jan. 18 [2007] of Sharif Hassanyar, the news coordinator of Tolo TV, who was held for 30 hours and released without charge. The questioning and detention came, as best we can tell, because Mr. Hassanyar had been in regular contact with the Taliban [a radical Islamic group leading the Insurgency in Afghanistan] spokesman by telephone, like reporters from most other media organizations, local and foreign, operating in Afghanistan. He thus ran afoul of another provision in the document described above, although this kind of reporting is specifically protected under Afghanistan's media laws.

Afghanistan Independent Human Rights Commission and various other Afghan and international agencies have documented other examples of harassment and violence directed at journalists around the country. Such violence often follows a contentious piece of reporting that targets a local leader. Hardly anyone is ever prosecuted for carrying out such an attack.

The Ministry of Information and Culture has attempted to limit footage of women on television. The media monitoring commission, chaired by Mr. Khurram, summoned our station in early February to formally complain about "skin" on Tolo TV. The minister was specifically referring to Indian music video clips showing women dancing provocatively while clothed in attire that exposed their shoulders, arms or legs (below the knees).

Although such clips are tame by the standards of much of the rest of the world and had already been heavily censored to conform to local norms anyway, the ministry said the videos had generated complaints from Islamists who considered them raunchy and wanted further censorship. Such complaints don't match our own experience at the station, where we are receiving many more complaints from young people who want "less" censorship of music videos than we already have.

Trouble has also been brewing at the public television broadcaster, RTA [Radio Television Afghanistan]. The Ministry of Information and Culture has been waging a campaign to take direct control of the broadcaster despite the fact that foreign donors like Japan and the European Union have been funding RTA on the understanding that it will be converted into an independent public broadcaster. Most recently, armed agents entered RTA's offices to forcibly remove key staffers who had run afoul of the ministry. The move prompted the resignation of RTA's director, Najib Roshan.

Far from a legitimate attempt to impose accountability on a public broadcaster for its use of public monies, the wrangling over RTA subverts the spirit of earlier agreements between Kabul [the capital] and the international donors who have supported RTA. Our government promised then not to use RTA as a propaganda arm. And the armed response is entirely disproportionate.

Independent Media Are Vital

Worst of all, draconian media laws proposed by the Ministry of Information and Culture could limit the media's ability to inform and entertain by, for example, declaring that certain programs run against "Islamic values." The term "against Islamic values" is not clearly defined in the text of the proposal or in any other laws, and added talk that the proposal would protect the "national interest" raises fears that it will become a tool to control all broadcasts, whether news or entertainment. The proposal now goes to the parliament, where it is expected to enjoy majority support in the lower house and perhaps the upper house. Mr. Karzai is expected to withhold his support, at least this time around, but perhaps only if international pressure persists.

Self-Censorship in Afghanistan

The young Afghan woman in a head scarf spends all day staring at other women's bodies and Hindu idols on her computer screen, then covering them up. It's Laila Rastagar's job to turn Indian and Korean soap operas into family viewing in this conservative Muslim country. Dual flat-screen monitors illuminate the 22-year-old's face in the dark cubicle as she draws a blurry square with her mouse to obscure a collarbone, then a kneecap, then a Buddha statue. She's one of a crew of such editors employed by Tolo TV, Afghanistan's most popular station, to censor shows in an attempt to balance its programming at the intersection of radical Islam, traditional values and the West. Television has flourished in Afghanistan since the hard-line Taliban regime was ousted in 2001. Eleven private stations and one state channel now broadcast in the capital [Kabul].

Kuwait Times,
"Afghan TV Stations Find Censorship Line Is Blurry,"
February 16, 2009. www.kuwaittimes.net.

These trends are attracting the concerned attention of a growing number of international organizations. Freedom House's annual rating of press freedom in 2006 showed a reduction in media freedom in Afghanistan for the first time since the ousting of the Taliban [from power in 2001]. Reporters Without Borders' 2007 annual report on press freedom notes that media freedom remains "fragile." The head of the UN [United Nations] mission in Kabul, Tom Koenigs, has voiced his concern about many of these developments, especially the proposed media law.

Afghanistan's rapid transformation from a political and economic basket case into a viable democratic state has been nothing short of miraculous. However, attempts to "control" the media—even if motivated by good intentions—will only hinder Afghanistan's development as a democracy. It is understandable that some within the government feel threatened by the Taliban insurgency, but the government must not abandon the guiding principles of democracy in an effort to win the battle.

"The sad reality about freedom of press in Afghanistan is that there just isn't any, well, except in name."

Freedom of the Press Is Not Improving in Afghanistan

Safrang

Safrang is the pseudonym of an Afghan student and blogger. In the following viewpoint, Safrang argues that no press freedom effectively exists in Afghanistan. The government interferes frequently in the operation of news organizations and seems set on restricting freedom even further. Safrang concludes that neither President Hamid Karzai, nor the government, nor even U.S. forces seem committed to freedom of the press in Afghanistan.

As you read, consider the following questions:

1. Why does Safrang say Najib Roshan resigned as chief of RTA?

2. According to Safrang, of what did the ANJU accuse the Afghan Ministry of Information and Culture?

3. According to the author, what actions of American soldiers further undermined the dismal state of affairs for freedom of the press in Afghanistan?

Says Mr. Saad Mohseni, head of a large media holding company in Afghanistan, in a recent [March 2007] opinion [op-ed] piece published in the *Wall Street Journal*:

> Despite the many challenges facing Afghanistan, the country can boast some major successes and perhaps none is more amazing than the success of its media. In name, at least, we now have a free press.

A Little Freedom Is Not Freedom

It certainly is refreshing to learn about "major successes" in Afghanistan. Except . . . well, what does it exactly mean to have a free press "in name"? That qualifier is a bit puzzling to us. Just to help put things in perspective, would it also be fair to boast of women's rights in Afghanistan and then add "at least in name"? Ditto a functioning democracy "at least in name"? How does "at least in name" protect journalists from intimidation or women from violence?

Truth is—and somebody else may have already delivered this truth in these colorful terms—that having freedom of press is a bit like pregnancy. You are either pregnant, or you are not—you cannot be a little pregnant; just like you cannot have freedom of the press only in name. The sad reality about freedom of press in Afghanistan is that there just isn't any, well, except in name.

Nobody knows this more earnestly than Mr. Mohseni whose Tolo TV, among other [media] outlets, has run afoul of the intolerant conservative temperaments many times over its youth-oriented programming. And this is what makes Mr. Mohseni's praise for freedom of press in Afghanistan a bit disorienting—because he basically uses the rest of the op-ed to chronicle, in such detail as only someone of his level of involvement in the matter can, the many ways in which the gestapoesque media monitoring commission of the Ministry of Information and Culture (which he describes in the op-ed as "the main center of anti-press activity") attempts to curb and curtail freedom of press and intimidate journalists. The ministry is also the main driving force behind a disturbing piece of legislation (Mr. Mohseni describes it as "draconian") which is expected to clear both houses of parliament—much like the notorious "amnesty bill"[1] did recently. The legislation is aimed at curbing press freedom under the banner of such disturbingly undefined and vacuous notions as "Islamic values" and "national interests."

More Restrictions

Elsewhere, the ministry has exerted its power through sweeping purges at the government broadcaster RTA (Radio Television Afghanistan) leading to the resignation of its chief, Najib Roshan, in protest; attempting to limit women's appearance on television; and summoning a television station owned by Mr. Mohseni's group specifically for its insufficient censoring of "skin" in its music entertainment programming. Separately, for a couple of weeks the journalist community in Afghanistan was rattled by the surfacing of a certain stern, official-looking document that basically told them not to print any headlines about insurgent attacks on their front pages, and not to undermine national security. And just today, BBC [British Broadcasting Corporation] Persian reported that the ministry has ordered the cancellation of an Iranian music band's performance because the group allegedly insulted Afghanistan's national anthem and the poet Rumi [a thirteenth-century Persian poet and mystic born in what is now Afghanistan].

In a recent statement Afghanistan National Journalists Union (ANJU) accused the Ministry of Information and Culture of attempting to transform the national media "into a propaganda tool in the hands of the executive branch," and argued that the ministry is overstepping its limits and acting in direct violation of the Mass Media Law of Afghanistan,

1. The Amnesty Bill of 2007 granted all sides in the Afghan conflict amnesty for human rights violations. It was passed by parliament, but rejected by President Hamid Karzai.

Afghanistan Imposes Censorship Around Election Day

The Taliban [extreme Islamist group leading the insurgency in Afghanistan] and the Afghan government escalated a war of attrition and propaganda on Tuesday [August 18, 2009], two days before the presidential election, with the Taliban unleashing suicide bombings and a rocket assault at the presidential palace and the government barring news organizations from reporting on election day violence.

The attacks ... provided yet another indication of the insurgents' determination to keep people away from the polls and undermine Thursday's election, which has become a critical test for the Afghan government and its foreign backers.

Carlotta Gall,
"Afghanistan Imposes Censorship on Election Day,"
New York Times, *August 18, 2009. www.nytimes.com.*

2006. The statement also points out the ministry's suspension of the Commission for Media Complaints and Violations, forcing journalists to directly refer to the General Attorney for redress of their concerns. The statement concludes by saying that the union is "deeply worried" about the recent measures taken by the ministry, and about the new challenges facing freedom of speech in Afghanistan.

On a related note, the recent news about American soldiers confiscating cameras and threatening photographers in the aftermath of civilian deaths near Jalalabad further undermines the already dismal state of affairs for freedom of press in Afghanistan.

It used to be that on his American trips, whenever asked, Mr. Karzai would affectionately joke about the toughness of the newspapers in Afghanistan on his administration. It turns out he might have just appointed the right person as his Minister of Information and Culture to whip them into line.

Periodical Bibliography

The following articles have been selected to supplement the diverse views presented in this chapter.

Atia Abawi
"Afghan Women Hiding for Their Lives," CNN.com, September 24, 2009. www.cnn.com.

Amnesty International
"Amnesty International Report 2009: Afghanistan," 2009. http://thereport .amnesty.org.

Jon Boone
"Afghanistan Passes 'Barbaric' Law Diminishing Women's Rights," *Guardian*, August 14, 2009. www.guardian.co.uk.

Dexter Filkins
"Afghan Civilian Deaths Rose 40 Percent in 2008," *New York Times*, February 17, 2009.

Michael Hastings
"Afghanistan: How 'Long' Really Is Obama's 'Long Road Ahead'?" True/Slant, December 2, 2009. http://trueslant.com.

Human Rights Watch
"We Have the Promises of the World: Women's Rights in Afghanistan," December 6, 2009. www.hrw.org.

Greg Jaffe
"Afghan Civilian Deaths Present U.S. with Strategic Problems," *Washington Post*, May 8, 2009.

Genevieve Long
"Press Freedom in Afghanistan on the Decline," *Epoch Times*, March 29, 2009. www.theepochtimes.com.

Franklin C. Spinney
"The Afghan Escalation and Women's Rights," *CounterPunch*, December 24, 2009. www.counterpunch.org.

VOANews.com
"Women Activists Call for Long-Term US Presence in Afghanistan," December 23, 2009. www1.voanews.com.

OPPOSING
VIEWPOINTS®
SERIES

CHAPTER 3

What Progress Is Afghanistan Making Toward Democracy?

Chapter Preface

On August 20, 2009, Afghanistan held presidential elections. Hamid Karzai, who had been president since 2004, defended his seat against Abdullah Abdullah, a doctor. It was hoped that the election would mark a new period of stability for Afghanistan. Instead, the election demonstrated the weakness of democratic institutions in Afghanistan.

One of the most serious problems with the election was violence. In the run-up to the election, Taliban insurgents pledged to attack polling stations and to kill those who came out to vote. Zekria Barakzai, deputy chief of the Independent Election Commission of Afghanistan, told James Lamont of the *Financial Times* in an August 19, 2009, article that the threats were part of "an organized campaign to disrupt the process." Officials were so concerned about the effectiveness of Taliban threats that the government "ordered a media blackout on violence during the presidential election . . . to avoid a climate of fear where people are deterred from voting," according to the *New Statesman* in a report on August 19, 2009.

On the day of the election, suicide and mortar attacks on polling stations were in fact reported, and many voters, afraid of violence, stayed away from the polls. This was especially true in the south, where in some regions "only a trickle of men—and almost no women—defied Taliban threats to bomb polling stations and cut off fingers stained with the indelible ink used by election monitors," according to Carlotta Gall and Stephen Farrell writing on election day in the *New York Times*. There was a steep drop in voter turnout nationwide. In 2004 voting rates for the presidential election were at 70 percent; this fell to 40–50 percent in 2009, according to an August 24, 2009, report on Vital Voices Blog.

Women faced especial difficulties in voting. To prevent women and men from mixing, women had their own polling stations. Due to threats of violence from Taliban, however, "Hundreds of polling stations for women . . . did not even open in some areas," wrote Carlotta Gall in the *New York Times* on August 22, 2009.

Ultimately, twenty-six people were killed on election day, according to a CNN report on August 20. The violence and low turnout of the election were serious challenges to Afghan democracy. The viewpoints that follow discuss other problems with the August 2009 election in particular and with Afghan democracy in general.

> *"The best way to get to legitimacy, accountability, responsibility, and justice is through a form of government that looks an awful lot like democracy."*

The Afghan People Want Democracy

Christian Brose

Christian Brose is a longtime speechwriter for former secretary of state Condoleezza Rice and a senior editor and blogger at Foreign Policy. *In the following viewpoint he argues, based on polls, that the Afghan people overwhelmingly favor democracy. Therefore, he argues, it is in the interest of the United States to help establish a democratic government, since by doing so the United States will increase its own legitimacy and contribute to the defeat of the insurgency. Brose concludes that democracy in Afghanistan is necessary to protect U.S. interests.*

As you read, consider the following questions:

1. According to Brose, the United States should not be trying to turn Afghanistan into which democratic countries?

2. What must a government in Afghanistan incorporate, in the author's view?

3. According to Brose, what percentage of Afghans want the Taliban to rule the country?

Kudos to anyone who waded all the way through my loooonnnngggg rumination on Afghanistan [a February 9, 2009, article Brose wrote in *Foreign Policy*]. Some actually have commented on it, particularly my point about continuing to support democracy. Here is Spencer Ackerman [a journalist who specializes in security issues]:

> [I]f the idea is indeed that the Afghan people are the center of gravity, they won't bandwagon away from the Taliban-led insurgency without having their material and aspirational needs met, so *some* degree of—for lack of a better term—Central-Asian-Valhalla-ness [referring to the idea that Afghanistan can be made a Paradise, coined derisively by U.S. Defense Secretary Robert Gates] is probably appropriate, even if you take the position that the core interest of the United States in Afghanistan-Pakistan is to eliminate [terrorist group] al Qaeda's safe havens. The question is *how much* Valhalla-ness? Christian [Brose], I think, doesn't offer a compelling argument for the necessity of democratization, providing instead a contention that such a thing is desirable. It certainly is, but the question is what's achievable and what's related to the national interest.

And here is [journalist] Dan Kennelly:

> I think a democratic Afghanistan is a worthy, wise and achievable goal. But we musn't fall into the trap of thinking that if, say, $150 billion per year isn't doing the trick, then surely $300 billion will. The time scale for successfully shepherding a stable and *democratic* regime in Afghanistan needs to be geological, involving the minimum amount of pressure on our part over a very long period of time.

Democracy and Prudence

I know this wasn't Spencer's point, but all this talk of Valhalla is a red herring, which Dan's argument reflects. Is there anyone who seriously thinks we can or should be trying to turn Afghanistan into Germany or Japan in Central Asia—ever, let alone in the near term? Of course democratic practices and institutions are going to take a long time to become durable in Afghanistan. So, what then? We should give up on it entirely right now? We should support some alternative political order? Which is what, exactly? If not, then all of this boils down to: Let's keep helping the Afghan people build their own democracy, but let's be prudent about it. Well, obviously.

All I'm saying is this: The [President Barack] Obama administration keeps talking about how it wants to "deal with the world as it is." OK, I'm all for that. And the world as it is in Afghanistan, according to [a poll conducted in 2008 by the Asia Foundation], is an overwhelming majority of people who want a democratic government. We don't want it for them. We're not imposing it on them. It's their stated preference.

The key question is Spencer's: Democracy is surely desirable, but is it *necessary?* One answer is that there has to be a government in Afghanistan, and most Afghans want it to be democratic. That seems like a pretty good case for necessity to me. But let's put that aside.

Democracy Is Necessary

Here is the general line of reasoning that gets me to necessity: My starting assumption is we need a counterinsurgency strategy to succeed in Afghanistan, not just a counterterrorism one. If that's the case, we need local partners to build a political order that advances the interests (most of all security) and redresses the injustices of the population, especially the so-called "reconcilable" members of the insurgency [those that may be willing to work with the United States and its partners]. What, then, should that political order look like? A few

A Survey of Afghan Views of Democracy

Respondents give their opinions on the statement: "Democracy is better than other forms of government."

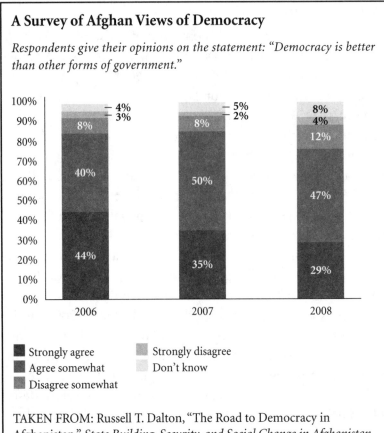

Strongly agree
Agree somewhat
Disagree somewhat
Strongly disagree
Don't know

TAKEN FROM: Russell T. Dalton, "The Road to Democracy in Afghanistan," *State Building, Security, and Social Change in Afghanistan,* Asia Foundation, 2008. www.asiafoundation.org.

basic things seem obvious and unarguable: It needs to be legitimate in the eyes of most Afghans. It needs to be accountable for understanding and helping to solve their problems. It needs to take the side of justice—so not, say, leaders who enrich themselves from the narco-trade [drug trade] while the average Afghan remains destitute.

If this is the kind of political order we need to defeat the insurgency in Afghanistan, then how are we going to achieve those goals without supporting some form of democracy? And by democracy I mean mechanisms that enable the popular will to be expressed and that root the Afghan government, at all levels, in the consent of the governed. In short, the best way to get to legitimacy, accountability, responsibility, and justice is through a form of government that looks an awful lot like democracy.

Yes, such a government in Afghanistan must incorporate and reflect Afghan tribal customs and culture, and we should be respectful and deferential to that. This point is key. . . . Still, it's hard to imagine the political order we need in Afghanistan and call it anything other than democratic.

One last argument for necessity: What makes the Taliban an insurgency is that it's trying to establish an alternative political order to the one the Afghan people freely elected to govern them. And we've all seen the Taliban's idea of justice and popular legitimacy. [The Taliban ruled Afghanistan from 1996–2001.] This helps to explain why another fascinating recent poll shows that just 4 percent of Afghans say they want the Taliban to rule Afghanistan. Since this is "the world as it is," supporting anything other than the will of the Afghan people, and thus a democratic government that reflects it, would be to preemptively surrender the single best value that aligns us with the Afghan population and differentiates us from our common enemies.

| "A feudal society in which women are still largely treated as property and literacy hovers below 10 percent in rural areas does not magically shortcut 400 years of political development and morph into a democracy in a decade."

Afghanistan Is Not Ready for Democracy

Thomas H. Johnson and M. Chris Mason

Thomas H. Johnson is a research professor at the Naval Postgraduate School's Department of National Security Affairs. M. Chris Mason is a senior fellow at the Center for Advanced Defense Studies in Washington, D.C. In the following viewpoint, they argue that Afghanistan does not have a tradition of representative democracy and, consequently, a president is automatically seen as illegitimate. The authors suggest that the dethroned Afghan king might have provided a source of legitimacy in a constitutional monarchy; however, the United States opted to give the monarch no role in government. The authors conclude that the only option in Afghanistan now is to downplay the central government and instead try to work with legitimate local leaders against the Taliban.

Thomas H. Johnson and M. Chris Mason, "Democracy in Afghanistan Is Wishful Thinking," *The Christian Science Monitor*, August 20, 2009. Reproduced by permission of the authors.

As you read, consider the following questions:

1. According to the authors, what do experts see as the sine qua non (indispensable ingredient) for counterinsurgency success?

2. Who was the "Iron Amir"?

3. According to the authors, the delegates to the 2002 *loya jirga* overwhelmingly wanted to install whom as the interim head of state?

A s the world watches today's presidential election [on August 20, 2009] in Afghanistan, Americans would do well to ponder the lessons of Vietnam.

The similarities are striking. The Republic of South Vietnam also held elections during the US intervention there, despite an ongoing counterinsurgency. Before American troops got involved, both countries had won upset victories over European powers after a decade of fighting, only to slide into another decade of largely north-south civil war.

Elections Will Not Establish Legitimacy

As historian Eric Bergerud has noted, the United States lost in Vietnam ultimately not because of its deeply flawed approach to counterinsurgency, as damaging as that was, but because South Vietnam never established a government seen as legitimate by a majority of its people. Experts agree that a government that 85 to 90 percent of the population perceives as legitimate is the sine qua non [indispensable ingredient] of counterinsurgency success. South Vietnam never came close to achieving such legitimacy, and neither, unfortunately, has post-2001 Afghanistan. In terms of incompetence and endemic corruption, [Afghanistan's capital] Kabul is Saigon [South Vietnam's capital, which was captured at the end of the Vietnam War by the North Vietnamese Army] déjà vu.

That's why we shouldn't read too much into today's election. Even if it were to yield a high voter turnout, have relatively few irregularities, and produce a strong majority for the winner, it won't give the new government legitimacy.

The father of modern sociology, Max Weber, pointed out that governments draw their legitimacy from three basic sources: traditional, religious, and legal. The first two are self-explanatory; by "legal," Weber meant Western-style democracies based on popular representation and the rule of law. And in this sense, political failure in Afghanistan was baked into the cake in the 2001 Bonn Process. [The Bonn Agreement was the process agreed upon to recreate the state of Afghanistan following the US invasion of Loci.]

In its rush to set up an overnight democratic success story, the [George W.] Bush administration overlooked Afghan history. Indeed, it was willfully ahistorical. That's tragic, because Afghan history demonstrates conclusively and beyond dispute that legitimacy of governance there is derived exclusively from Weber's first two sources: traditional (in the form of the monarchy and tribal patriarchies) and religious. Either there has been a king, or religious leadership, or a leader validated by the caliphate [the original Islamic government system] (or afterwards by indigenous religious polities).

Often in Afghan history, legitimacy thus derived has been reinforced by other means, usually coercive and often brutal. For example, the rule of Amir Abdur Rahman [Khan], "The Iron Amir," (1880–1901) and that of the Taliban [extreme Islamist group now leading the insurgency] (1996–2001) were predicated on accepted sources of legitimacy of governance (dynastic and religious, respectively), but reinforced by totalitarian methods. These two examples make the point that legitimacy should not be conflated with popularity: Having the authority to rule is quite distinct from being a popular ruler. American presidents, for example, are always legitimate leaders, but not always popular ones.

Western Democracy Does Not Fit in Afghanistan

Anybody that knows the history of Afghanistan will recognize the fact that they've practiced pure Greek democracy at the village level for two millennia. There's almost an American arrogance here thinking that we could come in and install Jeffersonian representative democracy on this country. It's also extremely important to recognize that the entire election fiasco of August [2009] has [set] any type of movement toward democracy back in Afghanistan.

Thomas H. Johnson and Greg Bruno,
"Painting Democracy on Afghanistan,"
Council on Foreign Relations, October 23, 2009, www.cfr.org.

There Is No Shortcut to Democracy

This historical reality poses a major problem for the US. Democracy is not a coat of paint. A feudal society in which women are still largely treated as property and literacy hovers below 10 percent in rural areas does not magically shortcut 400 years of political development and morph into a democracy in a decade. The current government of Afghanistan's claim to legitimacy is based entirely on a legal source—winning an election. Yet this has no historical basis for legitimizing Afghan rule. The winner of today's election will largely be seen as illegitimate *because* he is elected.

The tragic mistake, which we warned against, was in eliminating the Afghan monarchy from a ceremonial role in the new Afghan Constitution. Nearly two thirds of the delegates to the *loya jirga* [a grand council organized to choose a leader or discuss matters of national importance] in 2002 signed a petition to make the aging King [Mohammed] Zahir Shah the interim head of state, and only massive US interference behind the scenes in the form of bribes, secret deals, and arm twisting got the US-backed candidate for the job, Hamid Karzai, installed instead.

The same US and UN [United Nations] policy makers then rode shotgun over a constitutional process that eliminated the monarchy entirely. This was the Afghan equivalent of the 1964 Diem coup [which overthrew the head of the South Vietnamese government, Ngo Dinh Diem, with compliance from the United States] in Vietnam: Afterward, there was no possibility of creating a stable secular government. While an Afghan king could have conferred legitimacy on an elected leader in Afghanistan, without one, an elected president is on a one-legged stool.

An American cannot declare himself king and be seen as legitimate: Monarchy is not a source of legitimacy of governance in America. Similarly, a man cannot be voted president in Afghanistan and be perceived as legitimate. Systems of government normally grow from existing traditions, as they did in the US after the Revolutionary War, for example. In Afghanistan, they were imposed externally. Representative democracy is simply not a source of legitimacy in Afghanistan at this point in its development. This explains in no small measure why a religious source of legitimacy in the form of the hated Taliban is making such a powerful comeback.

As was the case in Vietnam after the Diem coup, there is little likelihood today of establishing a strong central government in Kabul which is genuinely seen as legitimate in the eyes of the Afghan people and which has significant public support across the country's ethno-sectarian divides. As a revision of the Afghan Constitution to restore a ceremonial monarchy is now highly unlikely, the only remaining option is to move away from counterproductive efforts to "extend the reach of the central government," which further undermine traditional sources of local legitimacy and resistance to the Taliban, and work instead to re-empower legitimate local authorities in a more decentralized state.

> *"The Obama administration is splitting a diplomatic hair in its acceptance of Karzai, declaring him "legitimate" but not necessarily "credible"—not yet anyway."*

Hamid Karzai Is a Legitimate Afghan President

Jake Tapper and Sunlen Miller

Jake Tapper is the ABC News senior White House correspondent. Sunlen Miller is an ABC News White House reporter. In the following viewpoint, the authors report on the White House position on Hamid Karzai's election to a second term as Afghan president after his challenger pulled out of a revote. The White House argues that Karzai is a legitimate leader because he followed election procedures for a revote and because he would have won the election if Abdullah Abdullah had not removed himself from the running.

As you read, consider the following questions:

1. What did White House press secretary Robert Gibbs answer when asked if there was a sense of legitimacy among the Afghan people for the Karzai government?

Jake Tapper and Sunlen Miller, "After 'Messy' Process, President Obama Congratulates Afghanistan's 'Legitimate'—If Not 'Credible'—President," Blogs.ABCnews.com/politicalpunch/, November 2, 2009. Reproduced by permission.

2. What did Gibbs say about Karzai's credibility?

3. Why did Abdullah withdraw from the runoff election, according to Gibbs?

President Obama telephoned Hamid Karzai at roughly 1:45 pm ET this afternoon delivering to him the best wishes of the United States for a second presidential term after an election fraught with corruption and accusations of illegitimacy.

"I congratulated him on his election for a second term as president of the Islamic Republic of Afghanistan," Mr. Obama told reporters as he sat in the Oval Office next to the prime minister of Sweden. "You know, although the process was messy, I'm pleased to say that the final outcome was determined in accordance with Afghan law."

Legitimacy Despite Irregularities

For weeks the Obama administration insisted that if the independent body investigating election fraud ultimately concluded that Karzai had received less than 50% of the vote, Karazi and his top challenger Dr. Abdullah Abdullah would need to either enter into an election runoff or some form of unity government.

At the G-20 summit in Pittsburgh on September 25, President Obama said "allegations of fraud in the recent election (in Afghanistan) are of concern to us" and he declared that "what's most important is that there's a sense of legitimacy in Afghanistan among the Afghan people for their government."

Today the White House was asked if there is a sense of legitimacy in Afghanistan among the Afghan people for the Karzai government.

"I have no reason to believe there's not," White House press secretary Robert Gibbs said.

Today the president said the fact that an orderly outcome—a runoff election ordered and agreed to, if not carried out—was "very important not only for the international community which has so much invested in Afghanistan's success, but most importantly it is important for the Afghan people that the results were in accordance with and followed the rules laid down by the Afghan Constitution."

The shift likely owes more to President Obama's belief that at this point the least worse option in the Afghan electoral mess is to accept Karzai, who won a significant plurality of votes in August even after disputed ballots were removed from consideration.

Mr. Obama made sure to underscore his dissatisfaction with the leadership of the president whose re-election he was re-affirming, saying he told Karzai that the American people and the international community want to continue their partnership, but he also "emphasized that this has to be a point in time in which we begin to write a new chapter" in Afghanistan's history, "based on improved governance, a much more serious effort to eradicate corruption," and more joint training of Afghan forces "so the Afghan people can provide for their own security."

"That kind of coordination and a sense on the part of President Karzai that after some difficult years when there's been some drift that he is going to move boldly and forcefully forward to take advantage of the international community's interest with his country, to initiate reform internally, that has to be one of our highest priorities," the president said.

"He assured me that he understood the importance of this moment," Mr. Obama reported. But, he said, he told him, "the proof is not going to be in words, it's going to be in deeds."

So how will this decision impact President Obama's decision on strategy going forward in Afghanistan?

White House officials insist they never were under the impression that the next president of Afghanistan was going to be the Second Coming of Thomas Jefferson; there were always

Abdullah Abdullah Criticizes the Election Process

Afghanistan's last presidential challenger, Abdullah Abdullah, dropped out of the race on Sunday [November 1, 2009], accusing the government of profound corruption and electoral fraud even as the [Barack] Obama administration rallied around President Hamid Karzai.

Mr. Abdullah, in an emotional speech to thousands of supporters here [in the capital Kabul], did not ask Afghans to take to the streets to protest or boycott the political system.

But he said he could not take part in an election runoff this week that he believed would be at least as fraudulent as the badly tainted first round in August, in which almost a million ballots for Mr. Karzai were thrown out as fakes.

Carlotta Gall and Jeff Zeleny,
"Out of Race, Karzai Rival Is Harsh Critic of Election,"
New York Times, *November 1, 2009. www.nytimes.com.*

going to be issues, they say, when it came to governance, corruption, training Afghan security forces, and expanding the president's power beyond Kabul.

The Road to Credibility

The Obama administration is splitting a diplomatic hair in its acceptance of Karzai, declaring him "legitimate" but not necessarily "credible"—not yet, anyway.

Earlier, asked if Karzai was the legitimate, credible partner President Obama and his team have repeatedly said the U.S. effort in Afghanistan needs, White House press secretary Robert Gibbs told reporters that "everyone can take heart in the notion that the laws of Afghanistan and the institutions of Afghanistan prevailed. President Karzai has been declared the winner of the Afghan election and will head the next government of Afghanistan. So, obviously, he's the legitimate leader of the country."

State Department spokesman Ian Kelly told reporters "legitimacy is derived from the government respecting the will of the Afghan people and obeying Afghanistan's laws and institutions. And what we're seeing so far is all of these laws and institutions being respected."

As for Karzai's credibility, Gibbs said, "nobody has ever made the accusation that credibility was going to be had simply out of one election."

The White House spokesman insisted "that would have been true, quite frankly, whomever got elected and whoever participated. . . . The conversations that now have to be had and continued with the Afghan government are the steps that they're going to take to improve their governance, to improve their civil society, and to address fraud and corruption."

"Now begin the hard conversations about ensuring credibility," Gibbs said. "We are focused on what has to happen in order to have a credible partner" in preparation for when U.S. troops leave the country, he said, so "when ultimately we leave, there's somebody there that can sustain the progress that's been made. Obviously, one of the things that has been talked quite a bit about in the Situation Room meetings is, how do we create an environment that best trains Afghan national army and Afghan national police as part of an Afghan national security force?"

Karzai Is the Choice Leader for the Majority

Karzai's legitimacy, of course, is not so obvious to everyone.

The first Afghan-run election, held in August, was riddled with so much fraud that more than a million ballots were thrown out by the United Nations–backed Electoral Complaints Commission. When Abdullah withdrew today he said he was worried fraud would continue. He had asked Karzai to remove the head of the Independent Electoral Commission; Karzai refused.

When it was pointed out to him that quite obviously Abdullah has some questions about Karzai's legitimacy, Gibbs said, "Dr. Abdullah made his own personal and political decision about this particular runoff." Gibbs argued that the investigation into allegations of fraud "worked, throwing out enough votes to require a second round, and convincing President Karzai to participate in that, which clearly was not by any means a given."

Obama administration officials argued that Abdullah was likely to lose Saturday's runoff election, and suggested his withdrawal was his seizing an opportunity to make a point about corruption.

Gibbs pointed out that even after the ballots were thrown out, "you saw that Dr. Abdullah trailed by a fairly large margin to President Karzai."

"So," Gibbs said, "I don't think there's any reason to believe that the Afghan people won't think this government is as legitimate as it is."

> "Afghanistan's fraudulent first round [election] undermined President Hamid Karzai's credibility both at home and in key countries contributing troops to the region."

Hamid Karzai's Regime Is Illegitimate

Peter W. Galbraith

Peter W. Galbraith was the United Nations deputy special representative for Afghanistan and was involved in exposing fraud in the 2009 Afghan elections. In the following viewpoint, Galbraith argues that the presidential elections in Afghanistan were hopelessly corrupt and that incumbent Hamid Karzai ensured that the second round of voting would also be fraudulent. Galbraith argues that Karzai's actions undermined his legitimacy both among Afghanis and with foreign governments that contribute money and troops to the Afghan regime.

As you read, consider the following questions:

1. According to Galbraith, how many phony votes were cast during the first Afghan election?

2. How does Galbraith identify "ghost polling centers"?

3. According to the author, why was he removed from the UN mission monitoring Afghanistan's elections?

Massive fraud in the first round of Afghanistan's presidential elections, held Aug. 20 [2009], plunged the country into a seven-week political crisis that gave the Taliban [the radical Islamic group heading the insurgency since 2001] its greatest strategic gains in eight years of war. As things now stand, the second round, scheduled for Saturday [November 7, 2009], will be even worse.

The runoff election faces profound challenges. Afghanistan's fraudulent first round undermined President Hamid Karzai's credibility both at home and in key countries contributing troops to the region. Electoral misconduct is one important reason that President [Barack] Obama is rightly reconsidering the wisdom of sending an additional 40,000 troops. The Taliban, which benefited from chaos created by the August fraud, now has every incentive to wreak havoc in the second round. Voters, many of whom risked their lives to vote in August, are understandably cynical when they see that their real votes were diluted by 1 million or more phony ones. As a result, turnout in the second round may be very low.

But the biggest challenge to holding fair elections in Afghanistan is the body administering them, the Independent Election Commission [of Afghanistan]. Aside from its name, there is nothing independent about the commission. Karzai appointed all seven commissioners, and in every important question, the commission has sided with the Karzai campaign. The commission chairman, Azizullah Lodin, has publicly said that Karzai won the first round and will win the second, statements that are among the many sound reasons that Karzai's opponent, former Foreign Minister Abdullah Abdullah, has demanded Lodin's resignation. There is overwhelming evidence that commission staff committed fraud, collaborated on fraud and knew about fraud that it failed to report.

A week ago, things in Afghanistan looked hopeful. After intense pressure from the United States and its allies and skillful diplomacy by Senate Foreign Relations Committee Chairman John Kerry, Karzai agreed to a runoff against Abdullah. (The bouquets tossed Karzai's way in the wake of the agreement were undeserved; he had been resisting the runoff even though it was required by the Afghanistan Constitution and an electoral law he himself had signed.)

The Revote Is Heading for Disaster

The UN [United Nations] mission in Afghanistan had announced steps to ensure that the fraud that occurred in the first round was not repeated in the second. These included the firing of 200 election officials responsible for polling centers with fraudulent results and a significant reduction in the number of polling centers, with the goal of closing what I call "ghost polling centers." These were centers supposedly located in highly insecure areas or areas controlled by the Taliban but that never actually existed. Although they never opened, the ghost polling centers produced many of the more than 1 million fraudulent Karzai votes in the first round.

In the week since the agreement, it has become clear that Karzai and his allies are determined to win the second round by any means possible, regardless of the cost to the country or the international military effort. On Oct. 29, the election commission announced that there would be more polling centers in the second round than the first: 6,322, compared with the 6,187 that the commission claimed had opened in the first round. It is a sure bet that almost all of these additional polling centers will not actually exist, but they will produce lots of votes. Many of the fired election officials are being rehired, ostensibly because there are not enough literate people available to do the work. As a result, Afghanistan faces a toxic combination of more ghost polling centers in an election administered by the very people responsible for the fraud.

The Taliban has announced its intention to disrupt the elections, and last week carried out a murderous attack on a UN guesthouse in [capital city] Kabul that housed many staff working on elections. Although these elections are described as Afghan-led, the election commission is heavily dependent on UN staff to carry out its logistical operations. Now, several of the UN staff are dead and many others have been evacuated for their safety, raising the practical question as to whether the commission is capable of pulling off the elections.

The UN Security Council gave the UN mission in Kabul the mandate to support the election commission in the holding of free, fair and transparent elections. But neither the commission nor Karzai has any interest in fair elections. Until recently, Kai Eide, the Norwegian diplomat who heads the UN mission, has taken the view that the UN had no authority to push the election commission to behave in a nonpartisan manner, even though the United Nations is paying about $200 million to hold the elections.

The UN Should Be More Active

I served as Eide's deputy and disagreed with his approach. With so much at stake for the success of the international military mission, I felt that the UN should view the election commission as the partisan body that it is and use our substantial leverage to insist on procedures to minimize fraud. Although ours was a private disagreement over policy, Eide lobbied for my removal, and UN Secretary-General Ban Ki-moon complied. Ban continues to embrace the laissez-faire approach, last week telling a reporter that the number of polling centers is entirely up to the election commission, even though everyone understands that more polling centers mean more ghost polling centers and more fraud.

Map of Polling Stations Where More Than 100 Voted and Hamid Karzai Won 100% of the Vote in the 2009 Afghan Elections

In the 2009 elections, more than 700,000 of Karzai's votes came from polling stations where he received every vote cast. Such voting patterns are considered a sign of fraud.

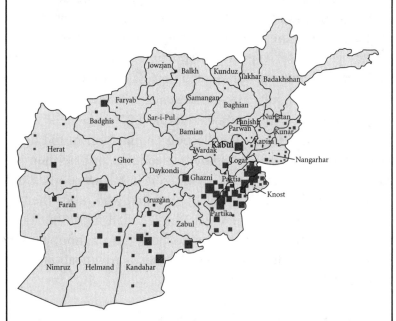

Squares are sized in proportion to the number of polling stations where at least 100 voted and 100 percent of the vote was for Mr. Karzai.

.1 ■ 20 ■ 50

TAKEN FROM: Shan Carter, Matthew Ericson, and Archie Tse, "Setting the Stage for the Recount," *New York Times*, October 16, 2009. www.nytimes.com.

Most recently, Eide has tried to take a more aggressive approach, even telling foreign diplomats he wanted Karzai replaced by an interim government (an unconstitutional solution that could increase cynicism in Afghanistan about the democratic process). But Eide is the victim of his past passivity. The election commission has thumbed its nose at the UN by increasing the number of polling centers and rehiring the corrupt election officials.

With less than a week to go until the scheduled runoff, there is not much the U.S. can do to avoid a disastrous rerun of the August elections. But the Obama administration should be deeply skeptical about whatever results are announced. When the election commission announced preliminary results from the first round, Karzai's total stood at 54% and Abdullah's at 29%. A separate, UN-backed Electoral Complaints Commission [ECC] examined just 10% of the suspect ballots and took Karzai's total slightly below the 50% mark needed to avoid a runoff. ECC insiders tell me that they believe a full recount would have reduced the Karzai total to 41% and raised the Abdullah total to 34%. Although the conventional wisdom holds that Karzai will easily win the second round, that might not be true in an honest election.

As things stand, it is all but certain that there will not be an honest vote in Afghanistan on Saturday. [No election was held; Abdullah dropped out of the running, and Karzai won by default].

| "The word 'corruption' has often been taboo in other countries. In Afghanistan the government has been frank and open in discussing its concerns about corruption and its commitment to fight against corruption."

Important Gains Can Be Made Against Government Corruption in Afghanistan

United Nations Office on Drugs and Crime

This viewpoint was published by the United Nations Office on Drugs and Crime (UNODC) for five organizations involved in development efforts in Afghanistan, including the UNODC, the Asian Development Bank, the UK Department for International Development, the United Nations Development Programme, and the World Bank. The viewpoint argues that, while corruption in Afghanistan remains a serious problem, the government has made a concrete effort to address the issue, and that further steps can and should be taken. For instance, the viewpoint suggests that the government should put forward an achievable action

United Nations Office on Drugs and Crime, "I. Introduction and Historical Background, II. Corruption in Afghanistan, IV. Achievements and Challenges, and V. A Roadmap for Action," *Fighting Corruption in Afghanistan: A Roadmap for Strategy and Action*, February 16, 2007, pp. 3–4, 14–18, 20–25. Copyright © 2007 UNODC. All Rights Reserved. Reproduced by permission.

plan, review the institutional framework of Afghanistan's anti-corruption strategy, and undertake more research into the exact nature of corruption in the country.

As you read, consider the following questions:

1. According to this viewpoint, what are some of the ways in which the Afghan government has specifically shown that it recognizes corruption as a critical issue?

2. How has the Afghanistan Investment Support Agency contributed to reducing corruption, according to this viewpoint?

3. According to the authors, what tangible measures can international partners take to reduce corruption in Afghanistan?

By all indications corruption (defined as "the abuse of public position for private gain") is a very important and quite likely a growing problem in Afghanistan. . . .

Corruption is generally considered to be a symptom and outcome of weak governance, in the case of Afghanistan reflecting in large part the legacy of a quarter-century of conflict and erosion of state institutions, irregular financing of the conflict from various sources, worsening tensions among ethnic and tribal groups, and the growth of informal/illicit economic activities. Hence in the Afghan context corruption has been intimately linked with the development (and destruction) of the state. Since 2001 [when the United States invaded Afghanistan] the burgeoning drug economy (combined with unintended adverse side effects of counter-narcotics efforts) and large inflows of aid have greatly increased opportunities for corruption, including, to some extent, through the revival of the economy (in that regulations and red tape provide scope for corrupt activities).

The Costs of Corruption

Corruption has multiple and severe adverse effects on Afghanistan. In addition to the direct financial costs of corruption (higher costs of contracts and public services, loss of public funds due to theft or misuse of government facilities and assets) there are substantial costs related to time devoted to corrupt practices by government officials, private businesses, and the public as well as, especially in the case of the security sector, the human costs (e.g., of threats, intimidation, victimization of people by security forces). Moreover, widespread corruption (or perceptions about the level of corruption in Afghanistan) deters and distorts private investment. But perhaps most important are the adverse implications of corruption, and popular perceptions of widespread corruption, for the effective functioning, credibility, and legitimacy of the state. A particular problem in this regard is drug-related corruption, allegedly involving senior government officials, which interacts destructively with corruption in the security sector (especially the police) and justice sector. And finally, corruption in Afghanistan, which is morally rejected on the grounds of being against the basic principles of Islam, further undermines the social fabric and erodes trust, possibly contributing to persistence or resurgence of conflict. All in all, corruption comprises one of the main obstacles to statebuilding and development in Afghanistan and, indeed, threatens the overall success of the ambitious program of political normalization, reconstruction, and development now under way. . . .

Anticorruption Achievements

Although corruption remains a critical issue for the stability and development of Afghanistan, it must be recognized that a number of important building blocks against corruption have been put in place over the last five years [that is, from 2004–2009].

First, government has consistently recognized corruption as a critical issue and has taken meaningful actions in terms of overall policies as well as some degree of institutional development. Although the government's commitment against corruption is sometimes questioned, it should be remembered that the word "corruption" has often been taboo in other countries. In Afghanistan the government has been frank and open in discussing its concerns about corruption and its commitment to fight against corruption. From President [Hamid] Karzai's speech at the Tokyo Conference in January 2002 to the I-ANDS [Interim Afghanistan National Development Strategy] prepared last year [2008], fighting corruption has been emphasized as a critical issue. In 2004, the government signed the United Nations Convention Against Corruption (UNCAC), and a law against corruption and bribery was promulgated. In the same year the General Independent Administration of Anti-Corruption (GIAAC) was established. The Afghanistan Compact agreed between the government and international community in January 2005 included anticorruption benchmarks. In 2005 the government introduced an "Accountability Week" where ministers have to defend their achievements. In 2006, a high-level Inter-Institutional Committee was formed by the president to look into administrative corruption and develop recommendations on how to fight it.

Second, some progress has been made in the area of public administration. A new Civil Service Law, gazetted in 2005, establishes (i) the principle of open competition and merit for all civil service appointments; (ii) the Independent Administrative Reform and Civil Service Commission (IARCSC, including independent appointment and appeal boards); (iii) the basis for a number of regulations and procedures to be developed (including human resource regulations and appointments procedures); and (iv) the Administrative Reform Secretariat (ARS) as the focal point for public administration

Corruption in Afghanistan Is Worsening

Afghanistan has been rated by Transparency International as the second-most corrupt nation in the world [as of November 2009], with public sector corruption worsening for the second consecutive year.

Only war-torn Somalia [Africa] rates worse on the Berlin-based organisation's Corruption Perceptions Index (CPI) of 180 nations.

Al Jazeera English,
"Afghanistan Corruption Worsening,"
November 17, 2009, http://english.aljazeera.net.

reform. The Independent Appointment Board has now processed 1,500 senior appointments using merit-based recruitment processes. Even though the quality of the process has been imperfect, this represents a critical mass of experience for the future.

Third, fiduciary standards have been significantly raised. This is the result of a number of actions taken by the Ministry of Finance in particular. The Public Finance and Expenditure Management Law, gazetted in 2005, establishes (i) a sound budget preparation framework with comprehensive and transparent documentation; (ii) requirements for accounting and regular reporting in line with international standards; and (iii) an independent review of the annual financial statements for presentation to the National Assembly. The Procurement Law, also gazetted in 2005, establishes (i) transparent and competitive procurement procedures with contestable mechanisms based on objective and verifiable selection and award criteria, and (ii) the responsibilities of government officials involved in procurement. The internal audit function is now being re-formed; moreover, since 2002 the ARTF [Afghanistan Reconstruction Trust Fund] Monitoring Agent has been playing an extensive monitoring role (akin in many respects to internal audit) vis-à-vis all recurrent expenditures in the core budget that are submitted by the government for reimbursement by the ARTF. . . . And finally, an assessment conducted by the World Bank of Afghanistan's performance in public financial management, using indicators developed by the Public Expenditure and Financial Accountability (PEFA) multi-agency partnership program, found that despite numerous problems, Afghanistan's PEFA ratings are now comparable to those of other low-income developing countries, which represents a considerable achievement as compared with the low base from which the country started in 2001–2002.

More Cause for Hope

Fourth, measures have been taken for sound management of state assets. A restructuring strategy for state-owned enterprises (SOEs) has been approved to ensure transparent management of the process of privatizing or liquidating SOEs. In the area of natural resources, modern minerals and hydrocarbons laws were approved in 2005, although the latter has shortcomings that need to be addressed. The government has committed to good governance in the underground resources sector. . . . However, these initiatives have been slow to be implemented, and as a result increasing levels of potential national revenue probably are being siphoned to private entrepreneurs and their powerful sponsors, with no record or tax, royalty, or license payments in accordance with legal provisions.

Fifth, some initial efforts are being made to put in place checks and balances. Although much remains to be done, the Parliament has now been established and can hold the executive to account. For the first time in 2006, the external auditor (the Control and Audit Office) was able to audit the government's accounts, and its report was transmitted by the government to the National Assembly. In the area of taxation, a system of appeals has been set up. Fiscal transparency has been enhanced by the publication of all annual budgets since 2003 and of monthly fiscal reports since 2005. Much interest in corruption issues has been expressed in Parliament, which held a workshop on corruption in November 2006.

Sixth, simplification has been initiated to reduce scope for corruption. The establishment of the Afghanistan Investment Support Agency (AISA) as a one-stop shop for business registration in 2003 has improved the enabling environment for the private sector, although much regulation and red tape remain, with associated risks of corruption, in other processes gone through by businesses. The tax code has also been simplified and the number of bands for import duties reduced. The government last year initiated a simplification drive to ease the burden of regulatory processes on citizens and businesses, and thereby reduce opportunities for corruption. For example, the process of getting a driver's license has been simplified, reducing associated vulnerabilities to corruption.

Finally, visible efforts have been made to prosecute individual corruption cases, although the results are not yet clear. While the motivation has been laudable, the weakness of the judicial system (as well as reported corruption in the justice sector itself) have hindered prosecutions. Meaningful progress could be achieved in the near future by removing corrupt officials from their government positions.

Challenges Remain for Anticorruption Efforts

While impressive in many respects, the progress made pales against the difficult challenges that Afghanistan faces in its fight against corruption. While in many areas institutional frameworks and reforms have been designed, promulgated, and in some cases put in place, implementation has often been slow or negligible. Moreover, anticorruption efforts have lacked a strong knowledge base and vision on how to address the problem. Some of the main challenges are summarized below.

First, a matter for serious concern is signs that corruption in many areas may well be growing (a hypothesis that needs to be confirmed by further analytical work), and that it may be getting embedded in regular day-to-day practices. Petty corruption associated with service delivery is very visible in Afghans' lives. In this context, the opportunity of the pay and grading reform in the civil service needs to be exploited to remove "poverty of officials" as a "moral" justification for corruption.

Another serious issue is the combination of high expectations and widespread cynicism and doubts about the government's commitment against corruption. This implies the need for the government to make credible commitments to taking meaningful yet feasible actions against corruption, and to follow through on them. But overly ambitious claims that exacerbate the problem of high expectations should be avoided as they would further weaken the government's credibility in the fight against corruption. While efforts to investigate and prosecute individual corruption cases are commendable, the considerable publicity given to them may unduly raise expectations, inevitably leading to disappointment and loss of government credibility later.

A critical challenge facing Afghanistan is the drug industry: It is certainly the largest source of corruption in monetary terms, which moreover carries serious risks of high-level corruption, state capture, and entrenchment of the drug industry and the insecurity (and weak state) which is the environment in which it thrives. Thus the success of Afghanistan's fight against corruption very much hinges on making progress against corruption associated with the drug industry.

Room for Improvement in Government Sectors

Corruption in the justice sector and security forces constitutes another major challenge, closely related to the drug industry in some respects. Corruption in these parts of the state directly affects both people and their perceptions (justice and security are commonly listed among the greatest areas of corruption in surveys of perceptions of corruption), and the credibility and legitimacy of the state. At the extreme, failure to contain corruption in the administration of justice and in the security sector could contribute to the success of the insurgency in the south.

Another serious challenge is the aid and other inflows of resources from the international community that occur outside government channels. It should not be assumed that these funds are somehow immune to corruption. In fact, there are allegations and perceptions of corruption, or at least serious waste, in donor-executed contracting processes, cascading layers of contracts and subcontracts (with overheads at each level), in international community expenditures on security (for example in the way that local security firms and guards are contracted), etc.

A key challenge is the recruitment and appointment process for government officials. This provides fertile ground for corruption when not handled well, but if done better could be a foundation of good governance. However, reforms in this area need to be fully informed of the local context (including historical background and cultural aspects). It would be better to aim for realistic and achievable improvements that work and have good prospects of being sustained.

Another challenge is reducing corruption in management of state resources and assets: underground resources, state-owned enterprises, land, and other assets (vehicles, equipment, etc.).

Corruption in revenue generation and diversion of state revenues from government coffers constitute another serious challenge to the government's fight against corruption which, through hemorrhage of revenue directly threatens the state-building agenda, in addition to constituting a burden on the private sector and taxpaying public.

A key challenge is bringing to bear government leadership in the fight against corruption and gaining coherence around an effective institutional structure for this purpose.

And finally, there is the difficult challenge of enhancing transparency and developing effective public communication of the anticorruption strategy, which must include strong efforts at awareness raising and behavioral change. In this context a parallel challenge is to develop the role of the "demand side" in controlling corruption, though stronger civil society organizing, building the capacity of media, ensuring accountability to and of Parliament, etc.

A Roadmap for Action

Building on the progress achieved, taking into account lessons from international experience, and responding to the challenges outlined above, a roadmap for action is laid out in this section. It would be unrealistic to expect that corruption, which appears to be increasingly entrenched in many parts of Afghanistan's public sector, can be quickly or easily eliminated. However, it is very important to make concrete progress both to begin to reduce corruption and to enhance the credibility of the government's anticorruption effort with the public as well as the international community. . . .

Solidifying the government's commitment against corruption. . . . The government could take some forceful, practical steps which would be meaningful in themselves and moreover signal its strong commitment to combat corruption.

An attractive option in this regard would be an action plan including a list of time-bound measures that the government commits itself to taking. While the actions included in the list need to demonstrate credible commitment, they should be feasible, and there is considerable flexibility as to which specific actions get included in the action program as long as, taken as a whole, they add up to something meaningful so as to enhance the government's credibility in this very difficult area. . . .

Shaping the Institution and Identifying the Scope of the Problems

Clarifying the institutional framework. Changing institutions takes time, and the institutional framework for anticorruption should be designed to help implement the anticorruption strategy rather than being fixed in advance. Nevertheless, there is an immediate need for some clarification of institutional mandates and responsibilities to reduce existing problems and tensions. Then a thorough review of the institutional and legal framework should occur as Afghanistan's anticorruption strategy is developed. Key aspects include necessary revisions to the law against corruption and bribery, reforms to improve the existing specialized anticorruption agency, and establishing a mechanism for high-level leadership, oversight, and coordination. . . .

Understanding better the context problems, actors, and dynamics of corruption. There is still much that is not known, or not known reliably, about corruption in Afghanistan. Moreover, the present context and historical and cultural background need to be taken into account in designing the anticorruption strategy and specific measures. Thus knowledge building and analytical work also comprise near-term priorities. . . .

Assessing vulnerabilities to corruption in key areas, taking appropriate actions, and monitoring. In addition to the analytical work outlined above, major efforts are being initiated to build concrete knowledge about corruption in specific government functions, agencies, and sectors, leading to recommendations for action. It is at the sector-specific level that much corruption occurs, including notably corruption in service delivery that directly affects (and is readily perceived by) the population, as well as in sector-specific contracting, regulatory, procurement, and expenditure functions. Thus it is at this level that much progress can be made through concrete measures at the sector level. . . .

Domestic and International Support

Resolutely pursuing key crosscutting reforms that will have substantial impacts on corruption. These include: (i) public administration reform; (ii) judicial reform; (iii) counter-narcotics strategy—a "smart" strategy against drugs; and (iv) strengthening of external accountability mechanisms (legislative oversight, community involvement, role of civil society—including media, private sector). These areas encompass important elements of the anticorruption work, although they also go considerably beyond it, and they are critically important and will have an important influence on the success of anticorruption efforts. Moreover, these crosscutting reforms can themselves be jeopardized by corruption, leading to significant dynamic interactions. Work is proceeding in these areas, including on public administration reform. However, reform of the judicial system has lagged and needs to be forcefully pursued, although much of it lies beyond the scope of the anticorruption strategy.

Developing an anticorruption strategy (as part of the ANDS). The Afghanistan National Development Strategy (ANDS), which is expected to be completed in early 2008, will include an anticorruption component, since corruption has rightly been designated as a key crosscutting issue for Afghanistan's development. The linkage with the development strategy is very important and underlines that fighting corruption should be seen in the context of the end-goals of the ANDS, which are peace, stability, poverty reduction, and broad-based economic growth. It is clear that Afghanistan needs to have a well thought-out, holistic anticorruption strategy that provides guidance as to the effective deployment and sequencing of the different anticorruption instruments as well as coordination, leadership, and institutional development. It is also essential that the anticorruption strategy adequately reflects the context in Afghanistan and responds appropriately to popular attitudes, while maintaining realism about prospects for progress. Ensuring that the anticorruption strategy is truly a government-wide strategy, with full buy-in and participation by all agencies that have significant roles in this area, also will be essential. These considerations point to the need for a diverse, multi-agency team to prepare the anticorruption strategy. . . .

Priorities for the international community. The international agencies involved will support different parts of the proposed action plan. More broadly, the international community should encourage and support the government in its efforts to effectively take on the challenge of corruption, while maintaining realistic expectations about the likely pace of progress. It is critically important that leadership of the fight against corruption remains firmly in the government's hands, with strong support from international partners in a fully harmonized manner. In addition to constructive encouragement through dialogue and provision of effective technical assistance, support from international partners can also take the form of tangible measures to enhance transparency in their own programs (for example disclosure of bid requests and contract awards and of audited financial accounts, in parallel with the similar actions undertaken by the government). In parallel with the government's actions to solidify its commitment, early efforts by the international community to ensure such transparency would have a good demonstration effect of its emphasis on good governance.

> *"The grave disconnect is that neither General McChrystal nor the administration have articulated in meaningful detail how this cancer of Afghan corruption will be treated."*

Important Gains Cannot Be Made Against Government Corruption in Afghanistan

Ben W. Heineman Jr.

Ben W. Heineman Jr. is a senior fellow at the Belfer Center for Science and International Affairs. In the following viewpoint, he argues that although the United States has called for a reduction in corruption in Afghanistan, it has not put forth any actual plans to achieve this goal. Heineman suggests that there may, in fact, be no adequate plan; corruption in weak states is extremely difficult to root out. He concludes that the United States needs to examine whether it wants to continue supporting the Afghan government if anticorruption efforts prove futile.

As you read, consider the following questions:

1. What percentage of Afghanistan's economy does Heineman report is drug related?

Ben W. Heineman Jr., "Corruption—The Afghan Wild Card," *The Atlantic Monthly*, October 2, 2009. Reproduced by permission of the author.

2. According to Transparency International, did corruption in Afghanistan increase or decrease between 2005 and 2008, relative to other countries?

3. According to Heineman, where must anticorruption efforts originate if they are to be successful?

As the President [Barack Obama] and other senior administration leaders hunker down in a windowless basement room in the White House to begin debate on future U.S. policy in Afghanistan, one of the most vexing issues will be widespread Afghan corruption.

The profound problem, as articulated by the administration's military and civilian leaders, can be simply stated. Corruption is a major cause of Afghan societal and governmental instability. Anticorruption efforts are critical to stability and legitimacy. Such governmental legitimacy is necessary to gain support of the divided, ethnically diverse people, and this support is a vital complement to military action against the Taliban. So, corruption must be swiftly and effectively addressed.

Corruption Cripples Afghanistan

But—and here it becomes vexatious—how can this be done by a weak, corrupt government during a dangerous insurgency, especially after a contested [August 2009 presidential] election marked by serious fraud? And, if corruption is not effectively addressed in a short time frame, does this undermine—indeed checkmate—the ultimate military mission as expressed by President Obama earlier this year [2009] to disrupt, dismantle and eventually defeat [terrorist organization] al Qaeda and prevent their return to Afghanistan by defeating the Taliban insurgency.[1]

1. The Taliban, an extreme Islamist group, were removed from power after the United States invaded Afghanistan in 2001. The Taliban have been leading an insurgency ever since.

To understand the importance of the anticorruption effort in Afghanistan one need go no further than actually to read the recent report sent to the President by the U.S. commander in Afghanistan, General Stanley McChrystal. Although the headline from the McChrystal report was his request for more troops, its deeper importance was his criticism of past U.S./ NATO [North Atlantic Treaty Organization] policy and his definition of the "problem."

Read his words on how central corruption is to his redefinition of the core issues which U.S.-Afghan policy must address.

- "We face not only a resilient and growing insurgency; there is also a crisis of confidence among Afghans—in both their government and the international community—that undermines our credibility and emboldens the insurgents."

- "Our strategy cannot be focused on seizing terrain or destroying insurgent forces; our objective must be the population."

- " . . . [A] properly resourced strategy must be built on four main pillars. . . . Prioritize responsive and accountable government . . . assist in improving governance at all levels . . . that the Afghan people find acceptable . . . on par with, and integral to, delivering security."

- "Criminality creates a pool of manpower, resources and capabilities for insurgents and contributes to a pervasive sense of insecurity among the people. Extensive smuggling diverts major revenue from [the Afghan government]. Criminality exacerbates the fragmentation of Afghan society. . . . A number of Afghan government officials, at all levels, are reported to be complicit in these activities, further undermining [government] credibility.

- "The most significant aspect of the production and sale of opium and other narcotics is the corrosive and destabilizing impact on corruption with the [government]. Narcotics activity also funds insurgent groups. . . ."

- "There are no clear lines separating insurgent groups, criminal networks (including narcotics networks) and corrupt [government] officials. Malign actors within the [government] support insurgent groups directly, support criminal groups that are linked to insurgents and support corruption that helps feed the insurgency."

- "The narco- and illicit economy and the extortion associated with large-scale developmental projects undermine the economy in Afghanistan. [The government] cannot fund its operations because of its inability to raise revenue, a situation made worse by the illicit economy."

Afghanistan's Rampant Corruption Is Not News

McChrystal's assessment echoes analyses by many others. Afghanistan supplies 90 percent of the world's opium and 30–50 percent of its economy is drug related. In 2005, Transparency International's annual Corruption Perceptions Index (built on its own surveys and on work by the World Bank, the Economist Intelligence Unit and others) ranked Afghanistan 117 out of 158 (with 158 the most corrupt). By 2008, Afghanistan was 176th out of 180 on the Index. (Disclosure: I helped found Transparency International [TI] and am a member of TI-USA's board.)

A discussion draft on fighting corruption in Afghanistan prepared in 2007 by, among others, the World Bank, the UN [United Nations] Development Programme, the UN Office on Drugs and Crime concluded after a review of governance indicators that "Afghanistan is fairly close to the bottom among countries in terms of the seriousness of the corruption problem."

The grave disconnect is that neither General McChrystal nor the administration have articulated in meaningful detail how this cancer of Afghan corruption will be treated. McChrystal's report talks vaguely about improving transparency both in the Afghan government and in international assistance to Afghanistan (which, he says, is also rife with "corrupt and counterproductive practices . . . too often [large development] projects enrich power brokers [and] corrupt officials"). He has all of one paragraph on rule of law. And he throws the problem over to a "cadre of civilian experts" who will be part of the buildup.

Similarly, the administration talks in general, conclusory terms about how to combat Afghan corruption. It recently sent to the Congress a draft of the "metrics" to be used in periodically assessing U.S. progress in Afghanistan (and Pakistan). A copy was published by *Foreign Policy* magazine. The measurements outlined in this short document are simply ends, not means: effectiveness of Afghan government in collecting revenues; public perceptions of Afghan rule of law at national, provincial and local levels; demonstrable action by the government against corruption; successful interdiction and prosecution of high-profile narco-traffickers.

Is There Hope for the Failing State?

So we are left with profound questions—which administration policy makers must answer and congressional and others must examine—about how it will address Afghan corruption. These more precise operational questions are of great importance because, as the last 50 years of post-colonial experience have shown, anticorruption, especially when it involves state capture and a strong kleptocratic class, is one of the most difficult and intractable problems in failing states like Afghani-

A Corrupt Mayor Continues to Run Kabul

The mayor of Kabul continued to run Afghanistan's capital city Wednesday [December 2009] despite being sentenced to four years in jail for corruption, raising questions about President Hamid Karzai's campaign to prove he's serious about tackling graft and bribery in the government.

Mayor Abdul Ahad Sahebi was found guilty . . . of awarding a contract for a city project without competition.

Amir Shah,
"Kabul Mayor Still Running City Despite Conviction,"
Associated Press, December 9, 2009.

stan, which lack transparent, accountable and legitimate institutions to order political, economic and administrative affairs.

National aid programs (like those in the U.S. and UK [United Kingdom]) or programs of international financing institutions (like the World Bank or the Asian Development Bank) or reformers in failed, failing and fragile states have all sought to address this intractable problem in the context of development agenda that focuses on both spurring economic growth and building institutional infrastructure. And there has been, of course, an outpouring of writing on anticorruption and development.

One conclusion is that processes . . . depend on each nation's history and culture, and they are slow, complex, fraught with difficulty and, thus far, often unsuccessful. Another conclusion is that anticorruption and broader development in failed states must start from within—outsiders can help but cannot command. Diverse writing from many disciplines elaborate these themes: development (e.g., Paul Collier, *The Bottom Billion*); economics (e.g., Dani Rodrik, *One Economics, Many Recipes: Globalization, Institutions, and Economic Growth*); political science (e.g., Francis Fukuyama, *State-Building: Governance and World Order in the 21st Century*); multidisciplinary (e.g., Robert [I.] Rotberg, ed., *Corruption, Global Security, and World Order*).

If "accountable governance" based on effective anticorruption efforts is one of General McChrystal's and the administration's "four pillars" of future Afghan policy (the others are better cooperation with Afghan forces, gain the initiative and focus resources), then the administration must somehow defy the history of many poor states, address this issue with the right resources in the right places and explain its anticorruption strategy in credible, not conclusory, terms.

But there is substantial reason, in the Afghan setting, to think that this pillar cannot stand, that the symbol of the once and future Afghanistan is not an energized and legitimized government dispensing justice but the garish "narcotecture" of drug lord homes standing amid the poverty of [the capital city] Kabul. And, if this is so, how do we craft, execute and justify a strategy that holds off the Taliban but, in effect, also protects corrupt Afghan instrumentalities of power.

Those discussions in the basement of the White House must be vexing indeed.

Periodical Bibliography

The following articles have been selected to supplement the diverse views presented in this chapter.

Business Standard	"Saving Afghan Democracy," November 4, 2009. www.business-standard.com.
Economist	"Afghanistan's Anti-Corruption Drive," November 19, 2009.
Economist	"The Debacle of Afghanistan's Presidential Elections," November 5, 2009.
Ivan Eland	"More 'Corruption' Is Needed in Afghanistan," Independent Institute, December 9, 2009. www.independent.org.
Malalai Joya	"The Big Lie of Afghanistan," *Guardian*, July 25, 2009. www.guardian.co.uk.
Bahlol Lohdi	"Karzai Discredits Democracy in Afghanistan," AntiWar.com, December 11, 2007. www.antiwar.com.
Jackie Northam	"Corruption Ignored, Deplored in Afghanistan," NPR (National Public Radio), December 23, 2009. www.npr.org.
Jackie Northam	"In Afghanistan, U.S. Success Depends on Karzai," NPR (National Public Radio), December 21, 2009. www.npr.org.
Fred Pleitgen	"Corruption a Way of Life in Afghanistan," CNN.com, December 18, 2009. www.cnn.com.
Ahmed Quraishi	"How ODA 574 Installed Karzai, and Afghan Democracy," International Analyst Network, August 30, 2009. www.analyst-network.com.
Alexandra Zavis	"No Easy Cure for Afghan 'Sickness' of Corruption," *Los Angeles Times*, Nov. 18, 2009.

OPPOSING
VIEWPOINTS®
SERIES

CHAPTER 4

How Should the Drug Trade Be Confronted in Afghanistan?

Chapter Preface

Afghanistan today is a major source of opium poppies, a plant that can be used to manufacture powerful narcotics like heroin. This was not always the case, however. In fact, Afghanistan's position at the center of the worldwide opium trade is relatively recent. It began only in 1979, with the Soviet invasion of Afghanistan. During the chaos that resulted, Afghanistan fractured and government control over many areas collapsed. Simultaneously, according to an August 2004 article on the Integrated Regional Information Networks' Web site, "harsh antidrug campaigns in Iran, Pakistan and Turkey [began] reducing their production levels" of poppies.

The result was a perfect storm. With the economy in tatters and opium in high demand, Afghans turned en masse to opium production to fund their fight against the Soviets, or simply to make a living. Over the next fifteen years of war, production skyrocketed. According to Matthew McLaughlin in a 2007 essay on Iranian.com, "production levels [of opium] jumped from 200 tons in 1980 to 1,570 tons in 1990 to 3,416 tons in 1994." In 1999, the amount grew even further, to 4,600 tons. Similarly, in 1980 Afghanistan represented 19 percent of the opium market; only four years later, it had captured 52 percent of global production. By 1999, three years after the Taliban took control of the country, Afghanistan produced 79 percent of the world's heroin.

In 2000, the Taliban government in Afghanistan instituted a dramatic ban on poppy production throughout the country. The exact reasons for this ban were unclear. However, the Taliban are known for their draconian punishments, and when they ordered that the poppy crop should stop, "No one dared disobey," according to Saleh Muhammad Agha, an Afghan farmer quoted by Barry Bearak in a May 24, 2001, *New York Times* article. Production crashed; only 185 tons of opium were produced in the country in 2000, down from more than 4,000 tons the year before. The amount of land under poppy cultivation dropped by 91 percent.

The decline of the poppy was short-lived, however. In 2001, the United States invaded Afghanistan and overthrew the Taliban. Soon thereafter, poppy production boomed again. By 2009, Afghanistan again dominated the world's opium trade, producing "90 percent of the world's total" according to Dexter Filkins writing in an April 28, 2009, article in the *New York Times*. The Taliban are thought to promote and tax poppy production, using the trade to help finance the fight against American and North Atlantic Treaty Organization (NATO) forces, just as they used opium to finance the fight against the Soviets in the 1980s. The Afghan government is also widely believed to be riddled with drug corruption. The following viewpoints present different perspectives on, and solutions for, the numerous problems caused by poppy production in Afghanistan.

> *"It can now be said that all actors in-*
> *volved in destabilizing Afghanistan are*
> *directly or indirectly linked to the drug*
> *economy."*

The Taliban Rely on Drug Money

United Nations Office on Drugs and Crime

The United Nations Office on Drugs and Crime (UNODC) aids the United Nations in addressing issues involving illicit traffick-ing in drugs, crime, international terrorism, and corruption. In the following viewpoint, UNODC argues that the Taliban aids and, in turn, receives a substantial portion of its funding from the drug trade. UNODC states that the Taliban relies on income from taxes on poppy farmers, taxes on drug shipments, dona-tions from large dealers, and other associated sources.

As you read, consider the following questions:

1. According to this viewpoint, in 2008, 98 percent of poppy cultivation took place in what region of Afghani-stan?

United Nations Office on Drugs and Crime, *Addiction, Crime and Insurgency: The Transnational Threat of Afghan Opium*, Vienna: United Nations Office on Drugs and Crime, 2009, pp. 101, 106–112. Copyright © United Nations Office on Drugs and Crime (UNODC), October 2009. All Rights Reserved. Reproduced by permission.

2. About how much does UNODC assert the Taliban collected in farm-gate taxation between 2005 and 2008?

3. How much money does the Taliban need per year to finance its operations, according to UNODC's estimate?

Insurgencies have demonstrated an interest in and capability of using drug money for funding, such as the Islamic Movement of Uzbekistan (IMU) in Central Asia and the FARC (Fuerzas Armadas Revolucionarias de Colombia) in Colombia. The links between antigovernment elements in Afghanistan and its drug economy have been well noted. It has become difficult to distinguish clearly between terrorist movements, insurgencies and organized crime (linked to the drug trade or otherwise), since their tactics and funding sources are increasingly similar.

Destabilization Tied to Drugs

It can now be said that all actors involved in destabilizing Afghanistan are directly or indirectly linked to the drug economy. Insurgents' access to the opium economy translates into increased military capabilities and prolongs conflict. Opiates also fuel insecurity across Afghanistan as groups fight for control of routes and territory. Finally, the drug trade also indirectly contributes to political instability in Pakistan, Central Asia and the Chinese province of Xinjiang (bordering Central Asia and Afghanistan). These are all consumption markets in their own right, but also transit regions for heroin travelling to Western, Chinese, and Russian markets, in which organized crime groups control distribution networks.

This [viewpoint] examines interactions between the Afghan drug trade, the Afghanistan-Pakistan insurgency and organized crime. The opiates trade is a major component of Afghanistan's economy, as it has been since the mid-1990s. Insecurity is correlated with the opiate economy, but disentangling cause and effect is difficult. Distinguishing insurgents from drug traffickers is a challenge when these categories overlap in many individuals and groups. These analytical challenges arise because the opiate economy is a central rather than marginal phenomenon in Afghanistan. It is an important source of finance for networks of corrupt government officials and for many insurgent groups.

The term 'antigovernment elements' (AGE) permits simultaneous reference to a wide range of actors that are inhibiting the development of the Afghan state. However, it also obscures the varying motivations of AGE and the role shifts of individuals and groups. For example, a wealthy southern landowner may occupy a local government post, preside over sharecroppers who farm opium on his land, and support the insurgency in order to protect his interests from government encroachment. This individual might be considered an official, an insurgent and a drug trader simultaneously. Faced with these category overlaps, it may be more productive to examine how different *behaviours* interact (criminality, insurgency and official governance), rather than how individuals interact. . . .

The Link Between Insurgency and Opium Cultivation

By most measures, insecurity in Afghanistan has increased. Insecurity has been rising across Afghanistan since 2005, primarily a result of the insurgency's growing strength and improved logistics. Afghan law enforcement and coalition forces are the most popular targets, but there have also been a substantial number of civilian casualties. In 2008, Afghanistan registered a record number of attacks, ranging from suicide bombings to coordinated assaults on military bases and maximum-security prisons. Much of the violence occurred in southern Afghanistan, but insecurity has also spread outward from the Taliban's heartland to cover a majority of Afghan provinces.

Areas of opium poppy cultivation and insecurity correlate geographically. In 2008, 98 per cent of opium poppy cultivation took place in southern and western Afghanistan. According to UNDSS [United Nations Department of Safety and Security], these regions are also the least secure. Even in relatively secure provinces, the areas controlled or heavily influenced by AGEs generally cultivate opium, such as Surobi district in Kabul province.

As it is illegal to cultivate opium, it is hardly surprising that cultivation is more likely to occur in places that the government cannot influence. This creates a symbiosis between insurgent and drug trade activity: Drug trading needs to prevent or respond to government attempts to enforce the law; while insurgency is dedicated to minimizing and destroying government influence. Cultivation is a particularly difficult part of the opiate trade to conceal, and is a primary livelihood for a large number of people, so the cost-benefit framework favors violent resistance more than, for example, the processing stage.

Primary sources of funding for insurgent activities are:

- Private foreign donations, including diversion and fraud by legitimate charities.

- Taxes levied on the population in areas under their control or influence.

- 'Pure' criminality—trafficking in drugs, arms and humans, among others; kidnappings for ransom and extortion.

In practice, locally levied taxes and extortion blur together. Some individuals in insurgent-controlled areas give willingly to the cause; others may do so against their will.

Forms of Taxation

Two forms of traditional taxation are of particular interest: *ushr*, a 10 per cent tax on agricultural production; and *zakat*, a 2.5 per cent wealth tax applied to traders.

According to the 2007 Afghanistan opium survey, almost all opium farmers in southern and western Afghanistan pay the 10 per cent *ushr*. Depending on the area, this goes to a mixture of mullahs [Islamic religious leaders] and Taliban [a radical Islamic group that leads the insurgency], but is less common in northern, northeastern and central Afghanistan. *Ushr* has an established social and economic pedigree, with the Taliban applying the tax systematically when it ruled Afghanistan between 1996 and 2001. UNODC [United Nations Office on Drugs and Crime] sources also reported that Taliban commanders usually receive the levy in kind, whereas a cash tax is usually given for licit crops.

The total amount of opium poppy production between 2002 and 2008 was 37,300 tons, with a farm-gate market value [the net value of a product when it leaves the farm] of US$6.4 billion. Of this amount, approximately US$5 billion was shared by southern (US$3.4 billion), eastern (US$1 billion) and western (US$0.5 billion) farmers. The remainder, US$1.4 billion, went to farmers in the northern and central regions.

Given that the Taliban have not held sway in the northern and central regions, it is assumed that farmers in these areas have not paid this tax to Taliban insurgents since 2002 (with the possible recent exception of Badghis and Faryab provinces). In addition, until 2005, the Taliban was not very active in Afghanistan and it is assumed that it was not able to levy taxes. To calculate the value of *ushr* to the insurgency, UNODC combined province-level price data with opium production volumes since 2005.

Between 2005 and 2008, the total estimated farm-gate value of opium produced in southern and western Afghanistan is US$2 billion. It is therefore tentatively estimated that approximately US$200 million (10 per cent of US$2 billion) was paid as *ushr* by farmers. Calculations based on UNODC field surveys suggest that Taliban insurgents receive 30–50 per cent of total *ushr* levies. This range is also chosen to account for leakage resulting from the tax changing hands, as well as the fact that [the] Taliban has not had total control in the provinces selected. At trader prices, this yields an estimate that Taliban insurgents collected around US$60–100 million in farm-gate taxation between 2005 and 2008.

In areas where groups other than the Taliban prevail, they also benefit from *ushr*. For the amorphous spectrum of AGEs as a whole, therefore, the total funding from *ushr* increases. However, it is more difficult to determine how much of this money is used for insurgent activity and how much is purely criminal income.

Furthermore, insurgents regularly apply *ushr* to all crops, not solely opium. Their total tax revenue is therefore greater than the numbers calculated for opium cultivation alone. In principle, reductions in opium cultivation would be expected to undermine insurgent financing only to the extent that the total value of farm production in insurgent-controlled areas drops. However, sustained reductions in opium cultivation would also be expected to feed through into reductions in opiate processing and trafficking; higher levels of the value chain from which insurgents also benefit.

Opiate Trafficking and Insecurity

The relationship between opium cultivation and insurgency is relatively easy to analyze: It is essentially a matter of insurgents maximizing the economic advantages derived from territorial control, while criminals benefit from insurgents' interference with law enforcement. However, roles and relationships blur further at the trafficking level of the opiate value chain.

One simple interaction is *zakat*, a 2.5 per cent 'wealth tax'. *Zakat* appears to be applied quite systematically, particularly on low-level traders. As with farmers, it can be presumed that *zakat* is more or less voluntary, depending on the trader's disposition. Similar to cultivation, the ability to apply *zakat* gives insurgents an incentive to host and protect trading networks.

A second simple interaction, again based on territorial control, is a fee for passage. Traffickers moving cargo through insurgent-controlled areas pass checkpoints that charge them. Functionally, this is no different from bribes extorted by police officers in areas of government control. It is not clear how systematically insurgents apply such fees. There appears to be a mixture of value-based taxation and flat rates, but in the southern region in 2008 UNODC received multiple reports that opiate consignments were levied at 200 Afs. [Afghanis, the currency of Afghanistan] ($4) per kilogram. This seems analogous to corruption among officers: Fees may be greater for high-value/risk shipments, but often there are standard payments for movement. In Taliban areas, such payments usually secure a stamp to allow free passage, although this obviously does not protect traffickers from extortion by any government officials, warlord militias, or bandits they may encounter. Moreover, the tax schedule of the Taliban is itself augmented by individual insurgent units on an ad hoc basis, with unsystematic taxes/extortion such as *baspana*, a so-called "assistance" tax levied in the name of war imperatives.

Roles become more complicated when insurgents act as protection for drug shipments. Some Taliban groups or leaders are involved in joint operations with drug traffickers, transferring opium or heroin to major dealers on the Afghanistan/Pakistan border and sharing the profit. At a lesser level, in 2006, UNODC research suggested that in the southern region

> an alliance has formed between drug traffickers and the Taliban where the drug traffickers provide money, vehicles and subsistence (US$4,000 + a Toyota vehicle + subsistence for a 10-man group) to transfer around 2 tons of opium. The amount asked by the Taliban was almost equal to the 2.5–5 per cent of the total value of the opium being trafficked. In return the Taliban protect them and do not interfere with their activities.

When the Taliban act as private bodyguards in this way, it is more accurately considered criminality rather than insurgency.

A Complex Criminal-Terrorist Network

It appears to be common practice for insurgents to levy taxes not in cash but in kind, which raises the question of how they realize the value of the opium collected. Barter economies are widespread and deeply entrenched in Afghanistan, particularly in rural areas and including the use of opium as value storage and reference currency. Insurgents can therefore exchange taxes collected as opium for subsistence needs. For higher-value purchases, large opiate traders provide cash.

In the latter transactions, insurgents are active participants in the opiate value chain, running from farmer to large trader—who then prepares shipments for export. From one perspective, they continue to act as parasites rather than value-adders. From a different perspective, they provide the nebulous but crucial 'public good' of a space without government interference, in which other opiate traders and traffickers can function more profitably.

In another area of the opiate value-adding chain, some Taliban networks may be involved at the level of precursor procurement. According to South Korean law enforcement, a recent seizure of ten tons of acetic anhydride [a chemical used in heroin synthesis] in South Korea appears to be linked to the Taliban network. A subsequent investigation by Pakistani agencies found that over 50 tons of the substance—linked to the same network—had already been shipped to Afghanistan's southern region disguised as disinfectant (hydrogen peroxide) from April 2007 to March 2008. These recent findings support the assertion that the Taliban network is more involved in drug trafficking than previously thought.

The murkiest arrangements by which insurgents derive funding from trafficking is the revenue provided by large networks. Previous examples of large traders like Haji Juma Khan suggest that such traders give sizeable but ad hoc donations to the Taliban. The apparently growing fusion between big drug networks and Taliban protection in Taliban-controlled areas indicate that these arrangements are likely to prevail throughout the network. In other words, whether individually or collectively, nodes of such networks are not subject to systematic tax schedules, but do, on aggregate, donate significant funds to the Taliban.

Finally, a different form of synergy between terrorism and the drug trade is evident in the dual use of trafficking networks for militants as well as opiates. Law enforcement sources have contended that in the province of Paktika (southeastern region linked to Wana in Waziristan, Pakistan) convoys are being used to smuggle drugs out and weapons (and fighters) in. Information on drug routes may therefore have counterinsurgency implications on the Pakistan-Afghanistan border.

To summarize, insurgency overlaps mostly with the minor, middle and macro levels of opiate trafficking, with the major-trader level left mostly to profit seekers. Macro-level involvement is the 'public good' of freedom from law enforcement. Middle- and minor-level involvement is the transfer of significant quantities of opium from farmers to traders and processors. This does not appear to involve insurgents taking the lead in transferring shipments over long distances or substantial cross-border opiate smuggling. At the major level, insurgents derive benefit from large but generally ad hoc donations from big networks. Lastly, when moonlighting as protection for major trafficking ventures, they are engaged in criminality rather than insurgency.

Opiate Processing and Insecurity

As with cultivation, there is geographical correlation between areas of insecurity and the location of laboratories. Processing facilities comprise the most geographically confined aspect of the opiate trade and their effects on security are narrower. While it is difficult to separate them conceptually from trafficking of precursors (in) and heroin (out), practically speaking, the facilities themselves create mostly localized insecurity. UNODC has no evidence that insurgents themselves manage processing facilities. Echoing the discussion of trafficking above, processing management would be a distraction from insurgency and would best be considered crime.

When in power, it appears that the Taliban would in fact levy taxes on laboratories "charging between $50 and $70 a kilo depending on whether the final product was morphine base or crystal heroin". Recently, an increasing number of reports, particularly from ISAF [International Security Assistance Force] and UNAMA [United Nations Assistance Mission in Afghanistan], have indicated that insurgent groups provide protection for processing facilities. This may be an opportunistic deployment of manpower by commanders and/or a calculated decision to protect a source of tax revenue. It seems that guards are paid in kind, that is, a cut of the processing output. Initially, this would seem quite inefficient, since each guard must then trade the heroin elsewhere. However, lab owners perceive some benefit in avoiding cash movements or payments and guards are able to take advantage of the widespread use of opiates as barter.

Nowhere is the entanglement of insurgency and crime more evident than in Helmand. To take the example of Musa Qala district, starting with repeated attacks in May 2006, the Taliban had nearly complete control for most of 2007 and the district became a hub for insurgent activity across southern Afghanistan. The Taliban established religious courts and presided over a flourishing opium industry, reaping protection money from traffickers and tax revenue from the harvest. At the very least, the Taliban were tolerant of the opium trade, with a new narcotics bazaar constructed and operating openly.

During the rise in insecurity and subsequent Taliban take-over of the district, cultivation figures for Musa Qala went from 1,664 hectares in 2005 to 6,371 and 8,854 in 2006 and 2007, respectively. At 12,687 hectares, the 2008 areas was double that of 2006. Without taking into account other taxes, if insurgents were able to levy *ushr* systematically in 2007, they may have earned some US$4.3 million.

Following the Taliban takeover, many Afghan traffickers previously living in Quetta, Pakistan and western Iran came to the district and lived in rented houses. There was competition and collusion in increasing control of local markets, including closer relationships with heroin laboratories, at least five of which were functioning.

In December 2007, the Afghan National Army alone reportedly seized 12 tons of opium in Musa Qala. Some interdiction operations also encountered Taliban protecting labs in August 2007. Afghan special forces operating in Helmand also reported that findings in opiate storage/processing compounds suggested a high level of insurgent/trafficker collusion. . . .

Insurgency Funding Is Derived from Trafficking

Between 2003 and 2008, the total export value of Afghan opiates is estimated at around US$18 billion (there is no data for 2002). Between 2002 and 2004, the Taliban had comparatively negligible influence across most of Afghanistan (with the exception of the southern and southwestern border areas) but this drastically changed after 2005. As of 2005, Taliban insurgents began to assert control over most of western (Farah and Nimroz provinces—Iran/Afghanistan border) and southern Afghanistan (Helmand, Kandahar, Uruzgan and Zabul provinces). Between 2005 and 2008, the total export value of Afghan opium is estimated at US$13.2 billion. Around 80 per cent of the opiates are trafficked via Afghanistan's borders with Pakistan and the Islamic Republic of Iran, which means that the total export value of opiates trafficked through Taliban-controlled border areas is approximately US$10.5 billion.

Similar to the *ushr* tax, there are a number of caveats to consider when attempting to quantify *zakat* and transit taxes. First, the percentage of taxation from drug traffickers varies substantially and taxes are rarely collected uniformly in any given area or region. Second, it is often sporadic rather than systematic. Finally, it is likely that drug traffickers are bribing other elements on the way to the Afghan borders (law enforcement and local commanders, among others).

Using a range that takes into account the uncertainty of the measurement and information collected, it is assumed that insurgents derive 2.5–5 per cent of the total export value (US$10.5 billion) as taxation from drug traders and traffickers. This means that between US$250–550 million was also expected to be paid in cash—or in kind—(or the equivalent in firearms, vehicles etc.) by drug traffickers to the Taliban in the 2005–2008 period.

In total, including the *ushr* from opium farmers (US$60–100 million in farm-gate taxation between 2005 and 2008), the Taliban is likely to have pocketed around US$350–650 million from the opiate trade between 2005 and 2008 through direct taxation of farmers and traffickers. Per year, this brought Taliban insurgents some US$125 million/year from opium/ heroin trafficking in Afghanistan. It is important to note that this excludes wages and taxes related to precursor importation and processing facilities.

Similar to *ushr*, the Taliban are not only taxing drug convoys but any vehicle which happens to cross one of the checkpoints they have erected along the highways they control. After 2005, some Taliban groups also became directly involved in trafficking of opiates to the Afghanistan/Pakistan border together with drug traffickers. In such cases, Taliban and drug traffickers apparently shared the profit. The net profit of the drug traffickers from opium/heroin trafficking is estimated at US$4 billion (besides bribery or taxation etc.), which would also significantly increase Taliban profits over the above estimation.

Afghan drug traffickers hand over the drugs to Baluchi drug traffickers at Afghanistan's borders (Helmand-Kandahar-Nimroz-Farah provinces) with Pakistan and the Islamic Republic of Iran. From there, Baluch traffickers take over. In eastern Afghanistan, drugs are trafficked (via Nangarhar-Kunar) into Pakistan's Federally Administered Tribal Areas (FATA). . . . . FATA is mainly controlled by insurgent groups like the Pakistani Taliban and other [terrorist group] al Qaeda linked groups. Negligible amounts of opium or heroin have been seized in FATA since 2002. At the same time, evidence indicates that Taliban elements are involved in drug trafficking, at least by providing security to the drug traffickers. The total value of the Afghan opium/heroin market in Pakistan is estimated at US$4 billion for the period 2005–2008. There is, however, insufficient evidence on the amount of profits these are generating in Pakistan to draw a conclusion.

Taliban Financial Requirements

According to some sources, there are around 5,000–10,000 armed Taliban fighters in Afghanistan, and around 4,000 Taliban were reportedly killed in 2007. Other estimates put the number of Afghan Taliban at around 30,000, including 15,000 Pakistanis. Regardless of the exact number, any insurgency must be able to replenish and provide for its fighters. Reports from southern districts indicate that the Taliban reportedly pay around US$200–500 per month to young locals, so called "tier-2 fighters." This amount is reportedly higher for tier-1 fighters [full-time Taliban fighters]. Across the border in Pakistan, a Taliban recruit reportedly earns PKR 15,000 (approximately US$200) per month.

There has been speculation that Taliban fighters are paid on a regular basis. Others thought the payments to be less regular, and more in line with the immediate needs of a fighter (such as marriage costs and leave pay). Taliban fighters are mostly constituted of small groups (not small armies) designed for hit-and-run attacks and led by an *amir* (commander) enjoying a large degree of financial and operational autonomy. Financial incentives for some fighters may therefore consist of payment for escorting a convoy, a portion of the booty from the commander, or a share of the *ushr/zakat* collected in areas under the group's control (at the commander's discretion). Depending on the relative poverty of an area, some warlords can even employ recruits for as little as a meal a day. In some areas where they enjoy support and can use tribal connections, the Taliban do not pay salaries and can recruit from a pool of willing volunteers.

On top of personnel costs, insurgents need weapons. Set against the potential income from parasitizing the drug trade—let alone other funding sources—these costs are modest. In Kabul, reliable reports indicate that a suicide bomber's family may receive between 600,000–1,000,000 Afghanis (US$12,000–20,000) for an attack. Other sources contend that, on average, suicide bombers are paid a more modest $3,000–4,000. With opiate income alone, insurgents can purchase thousands of weapons, fund hundreds of suicide attacks and retain thousands of fighters.

It is estimated that the Taliban need between $800 million and $1 billion per year to finance their operations. Based on the calculations above, 10–15 per cent of their funding could be drawn from the Afghan opiate trade—ignoring any revenue from trafficking through Pakistan that may find its way into Taliban coffers. This is somewhat less than the minimum percentage suggested by some ISAF officials, which ranged from 20–40 per cent of the Afghan Taliban's total income.

I *"The roots of Afghanistan's upsurge in drug production since 2001 are directly related to U.S. policies and the government that was installed in the wake of the invasion."*

Drug Money Does Not Go Primarily to the Taliban

Julien Mercille

Julien Mercille is a contributor to Foreign Policy in Focus *and a lecturer in U.S. foreign policy and geopolitics at University College Dublin, Ireland. In the following viewpoint, he argues that the Taliban get most of their money from sources other than the drug trade. In addition, he says that the drug trade has been encouraged in large part by the Afghan government, which is supported by the United States. Mercille concludes that Western nations and U.S. allies are just as much to blame for the flourishing Afghan drug trade as the Taliban.*

As you read, consider the following questions:

1. How much of the Taliban's funding comes from drugs, in UNODC's estimate?

Julien Mercille, "UN Report Misleading on Afghanistan's Drug Problem," *Foreign Policy in Focus*, November 5, 2009. Copyright © 2009 Institute for Policy Studies. Reproduced by permission.

2. How did a UNODC official respond when Mercille asked what percentage of total drug income in Afghanistan was captured by government officials?

3. What does the author assert is the world's deadliest drug, and how many people does it kill every year?

As President [Barack] Obama and his advisors debate future troop levels for Afghanistan [in November 2009], a new report by the UN [United Nations] Office on Drugs and Crime (UNODC) muddies the water on one of the most important issues in the debate—the effects of Afghanistan's drug production.

The report, entitled *Addiction, Crime and Insurgency: The Transnational Threat of Afghan Opium*, gives the false impression that the Taliban [the radical Islamists who lead the insurgency in Afghanistan] are the main culprits behind Afghanistan's skyrocketing drug production. It also implies that drugs are the main reason why the Taliban are gaining in strength, absolving the United States and NATO [North Atlantic Treaty Organization] of their own responsibility in fomenting the insurgency.

Drugs Are Not the Result or the Cause of Insurgency

In fact, the United States and its Afghan allies bear a large share of responsibility for the drug industry's dramatic expansion since the invasion. Buried deep in the report, its authors admit that reduced levels of drug production would have little effect on the insurgency's vigor.

The following annotation rebuffs some of the report's main assertions, puts in perspective the Taliban's role in the opium economy, and highlights U.S./NATO responsibility for its expansion and potential reduction.

Taliban insurgents draw some US$125 million annually from drugs, which is *more money than ten years ago, [and as a re-*

sult] the perfect storm of drugs and terrorism, that has struck the Afghan/Pakistani border for years, may be heading towards Central Asia. A big part of the region could be engulfed in large-scale terrorism, endangering its massive energy resources.

These claims are supposed to make us shudder in the face of an impending narco-terrorist seizure of a large chunk of the world's energy resources. UNODC states that a decade ago the Taliban earned $85 million per year from drugs, but that since 2005 this figure has jumped to $125 million. Although this is pitched as a significant increase, the Taliban play a more minor role in the opium economy than UNODC would have us believe and drug money is probably a secondary source of funding for them. Indeed, the report estimates that only 10–15% of Taliban funding is drawn from drugs and 85% comes from "non-opium sources."

The total revenue generated by opiates within Afghanistan is about $3.4 billion per year. Of this figure, according to UNODC, the Taliban get only 4% of the sum. Farmers, meanwhile, get 21%.

The Afghan Government and Opiates

And the remaining 75%? [Terrorist group] al Qaeda? No: The report specifies that it "does not appear to have a direct role in the Afghan opiates trade," although it may participate in "low-level drugs and/or arms smuggling" along the Pakistani border.

Instead, the remaining 75% is captured by government officials, the police, local and regional power brokers and traffickers—in short, many of the groups now supported (or tolerated) by the United States and NATO are important actors in the drug trade.

The *New York Times* recently revealed that Ahmed Wali Karzai, [Afghan] President Hamid Karzai's brother, has long been on the CIA [Central Intelligence Agency] payroll, in addition to his probable shady dealings in drugs. But this is only the tip of the iceberg, as U.S. and NATO forces have long supported warlords, commanders, and illegal militias with a record of human rights abuses and involvement in narcotics. A former CIA officer said that "Virtually every significant Afghan figure has had brushes with the drug trade." According to a New York University report, General Nazri Mahmad, a warlord who "control[s] a significant portion of the province's lucrative opium industry," has the contract to provide security for the German Provincial Reconstruction Team.

UNODC insists on making the Taliban-drugs connection front-page news while not chasing with the same intensity those supported by Washington. The agency seems to be acting as an enabler of U.S./NATO policies in Afghanistan.

When I asked the UNODC official who supervised the report what percentage of total drug income in Afghanistan was captured by government officials, the reply was quick: "We don't do that, I don't know."

Instead of pointing a finger directly at the U.S./NATO-backed government, the report gives the impression that the problem lies mostly with rotten apples who threaten an otherwise well-intentioned government.

But the roots of Afghanistan's upsurge in drug production since 2001 are directly related to U.S. policies and the government that was installed in the wake of the invasion. The United States attacked Afghanistan in 2001, in alliance with anti-Taliban warlords and drug lords, showering them with millions of dollars and other forms of support. The empowerment and enrichment of the warlords with whom the U.S. allied itself enabled them to tax and protect opium traffickers, leading to the quick resumption of opium production after the hiatus of the 2000 Taliban ban.[1]

1. The Taliban controlled Afghanistan from 1996–2001. During that time, they put in place an effective ban on opium production.

To blame "corruption" and "criminals" for the state of affairs is to ignore the direct and predictable effects of U.S. policies, which have simply followed a historical pattern of toleration and empowerment of local drug lords in the pursuit of broader foreign policy objectives, as [historian] Alfred McCoy and others have documented in detail.

Impunity for drug lords and warlords continues: A U.S. Senate report noted in August that no major traffickers have been arrested in Afghanistan since 2006, and that successful prosecutions of significant traffickers are often overturned by a simple bribe or protection from above, revealing counternarcotics efforts to be deficient at best.

Identifying drugs as the main cause behind Taliban advances absolves the U.S./NATO of their own responsibility in fomenting the insurgency: Their very presence in the country, as well as their destructive attacks on civilians account for a good deal of the recent increase in popular support for the Taliban.

Eliminating Drugs Would Have Little Effect

In fact, buried deep in the report, its authors admit that reducing drug production would have only "minimal impact on the insurgency's strategic threat." The Taliban receive "significant funding from private donors all over the world," a contribution which "dwarfs" drug money. Although the report will be publicized by many as a vindication of calls to target the opium economy in order to weaken the Taliban, the authors themselves are not convinced of the validity of this argument.

> Of the $65 billion turnover of the global market for opiates, only 5–10% ($3–5 billion) is estimated to be laundered by informal banking systems. The rest is laundered through legal trade activities and the banking system.

This is an important claim that points to the enormous amounts of drug money swallowed by the world financial system, including Western banks.

Everyone Is Involved in the Drug Trade

When it's harvest time in the poppy fields of Kandahar, dust-covered Taliban fighters pull up on their motorbikes to collect a 10 percent tax on the crop. Afghan police arrive in Ford Ranger pickups—bought with U.S. aid money—and demand their cut of the cash in exchange for promises to skip the farms during annual eradication.

Then, usually late one afternoon, a drug trafficker will roll up in his Toyota Land Cruiser with black-tinted windows and send a footman to pay the farmers in cash. The farmers never see the boss, but they suspect that he's a local power broker who has ties to the U.S.-backed Afghan government.

Everyone wants a piece of the action, said farmer Abdul Satar, a thin man with rough hands who tends about half an acre of poppy just south of Kandahar. "There is no one to complain to," he said, sitting in the shade of an orange tree. "Most of the government officials are involved."

Afghanistan produces more than 90 percent of the world's opium, which was worth some $3.4 billion to Afghan exporters last year [2008]. For a cut of that, Afghan officials open their highways to opium and heroin trafficking, allow public land to be used for growing opium poppies and protect drug dealers.

Tom Lasseter,
"Afghan Drug Trade Thrives
with Help, and Neglect, of Officials,"
McClatchy Newspapers, May 10, 2009.
www.mcclatchydc.com.

The report says that over the last seven years (2002–2008), the transnational trade in Afghan opiates resulted in worldwide sales of $400–$500 billion (retail value). Only 5–10% of this is estimated to be laundered by informal banking systems (such as *hawala* [a Middle Eastern banking system]). The remainder is laundered through the legal economy, and importantly, through Western banks.

In fact, Antonio Maria Costa [executive director of UN-ODC] was quoted as saying that drug money may have recently rescued some failing banks [amidst the 2008–09 global financial crisis]: "interbank loans were funded by money that originated from drug trade and other illegal activities," and there were "signs that some banks were rescued in that way." "At a time of major bank failures, *money doesn't smell*, bankers seem to believe," he wrote in UNODC's *World Drug Report 2009* (emphasis in original).

The Deadliest Drug

> Afghanistan has the world monopoly of opium cultivation (92%), the raw material for the world's deadliest drug— heroin, [which is] causing up to 100,000 deaths per year.

Tobacco is the world's deadliest drug, not heroin. The former kills about 5 million people every year. According to the WHO [World Health Organization], if present tobacco consumption patterns continue, the number of deaths will increase to 10 million by the year 2020. Some 70% of these will be in developing countries, which are the main target of the tobacco industry's marketing ploys. So why does the Taliban get more flak than tobacco companies?

The report estimates there are 16 million opiate users across the world, with the main consumer market being Europe, valued at $20 billion. Europeans are thus the main source of funding for the Afghan drug industry and their governments share a significant part of responsibility for failing to decrease demand and provide more treatment services within their own borders. Lowering drug use in Europe would contribute significantly to reducing the scale of the problem in Afghanistan.

Moreover, the report notes that NATO member Turkey is a "central hub" through which Afghan opiates reach Europe. Perhaps NATO should direct its efforts towards its own members before targeting the Taliban.

> Some Taliban networks may be involved at the level of precursor procurement. These recent findings support the assertion that the Taliban network is more involved in drug trafficking than previously thought.

Yes, the Taliban surely take a cut out of the precursor trade (the chemicals needed to refine opium into products like heroin and morphine).

However, Western countries and some of their allies are also involved: The report identified "Europe, China, and the Russian Federation" as "major acetic anhydride sources for Afghanistan." For instance, 220 liters of acetic anhydride were intercepted this year at [Afghan capital city] Kabul airport, apparently originating from France. In recent years, chemicals have also been shipped from or via the Republic of Korea and UNODC's *Afghan Opium Survey, 2008* pointed to Germany as a source of precursors.

It is unclear what the total value of the Afghan trade in chemical precursors is, but from the report's data it can be inferred that the retail value of just one precursor, acetic anhydride, was about $450 million this year. Part of that money goes back to Western chemical corporations in the form of profits. Tighter safeguards should be in place on these products.

Opium and Insecurity

Areas of opium poppy cultivation and insecurity correlate geographically. In 2008, 98% of opium poppy cultivation took place in southern and western Afghanistan, the least secure regions.

UNODC associates drugs with the Taliban by pointing to the fact that most poppy cultivation takes places in regions where the Taliban are concentrated. Maps show "poppy-free" provinces in the north and a concentration of cultivation in the southern provinces, linking the Taliban with drugs.

It is true that cultivation is concentrated in the south, but such maps obscure the fact that there is plenty of drug money in the north, a region over which the Afghan government has more control. For instance, Balkh province may be poppy-free, but its center, Mazar-i-Sharif, is awash in drug money. Nangarhar was also poppy-free in 2008, although it still remains a province where a large amount of opiates is trafficked.

Some Western officials are now implying that political elites in northern Afghanistan are engaging in successful counter-narcotics while the southern drug economy expands. But the fact is that although the commanders who control northern Afghanistan today may have eliminated cultivation, none have moved against trafficking. Most of them continue to profit from it, and some are believed to have become millionaires.

"With no heroin to fund terrorism and subvert the economies and political systems of Afghanistan and Pakistan, the American agenda could take a huge leap forward."

The United States Must Eradicate Poppy Crops in Afghanistan

Rachel Ehrenfeld

Rachel Ehrenfeld has a PhD in criminology from Hebrew University School of Law and is director of the American Center for Democracy. She is also the author of Funding Evil: How Terrorism Is Financed—and How to Stop It. *In the following viewpoint, she argues that the Taliban and other terrorist groups rely on poppy growth and narcotics for funding. Rather than send more troops, therefore, Ehrenfeld contends that the Barack Obama administration should aggressively eradicate poppies, using mycoherbicides derived from fungi. This would cut off funds to the Taliban and would free up U.S. money used to fight drugs, thus making these resources available to directly fight terrorism, Ehrenfeld concludes.*

Rachel Ehrenfeld, "Stop the Afghan Drug Trade, Stop Terrorism," Forbes.com, February 26, 2009. Copyright © 2010 Forbes, Inc. Reprinted by Permission of Forbes Media LLC.

As you read, consider the following questions:

1. According to Drug Enforcement Administration figures, how does the cost of a ton of heroin compare to the cost of a ton of oil?

2. Why did the British drug eradication effort in Afghanistan fail, in Ehrenfeld's opinion?

3. Why does the author assert that the George W. Bush administration failed to conduct efficacy studies of mycoherbicides?

"The fight against drugs is actually the fight for Afghanistan," said Afghan President Hamid Karzai when he took office in 2002. Judging by the current situation, Afghanistan is losing.

To win, the link between narcotics and terrorism must be severed. That is the necessary condition for a successful strategy to undermine the growing influence of al-Qaida, the Taliban and radical Muslim groups in Afghanistan and Pakistan.

It is all about money—more precisely, drug money. The huge revenues from the heroin trade fill the coffers of the terrorists and thwart any attempt to stabilize the region.

Though not traded on any stock exchange, heroin is one of the most valuable commodities in the world today. While a ton of crude oil costs less than $290, a ton of heroin costs $67 million in Europe and between $360 million and $900 million in New York, according to estimates based on recent Drug Enforcement Administration figures.

Since its liberation from Taliban rule, Afghanistan's opium production has gone from 640 tons in 2001 to 8,200 tons in 2007. Afghanistan now supplies over 93% of the global opiate market.

"This is a source of income for the warlords and regional factions to pay their soldiers," warned former Afghan Interior Minister Ali Ahmad Jalali in a May 2005 interview with Reuters. "The terrorists are funding their operations through illicit drug trade, so they are all interlinked."

In 2004, the G8 designated Britain to lead counter-narcotics efforts in Afghanistan. Its three-year eradication policy was designed specifically not to alienate the local population. It dictated the crop eradication be done "by hand." Moreover, the British entrusted the provincial governors with the eradication process, even though Afghan provincial governors, many of whom are powerful warlords, have been engaged in the drug trade for decades. Not surprisingly, the eradication effort failed miserably.

The exponential growth in narco-terrorism in Afghanistan led to a well-entrenched narco-economy, strengthening the power of tribal warlords, the Taliban and al-Qaida. The growing violence led NATO leaders, who met in Budapest in October 2008, to agree to allow their military forces to strike the drug traffickers. However, NATO troops were not ordered to attack; in fact, NATO's European allies are "averse" to drug eradication programs for fear of alienating the local population and because of the risks associated with such operations.

Though Afghan opium production shrank a little to 7,200 tons in 2008, it still accounts for 97% of the country's per-capita annual GDP, or $303 of $310. Yet Afghan heroin is worth $3.6 billion to $6.4 billion on the streets of most Western nations.

According to the latest report of the International Narcotics Control Board, the Taliban's income for 2007 from morphine base and heroin production is estimated between $259 million and $518 million, up from just $28 million in 2005. This provides more than enough to fund the most sophisticated weapons, training camps, operational and even public relations funds, and plenty of bribes to local tribes' chieftains and politicians.

While no one expects Afghanistan to become a peaceful, self-sustaining democracy overnight, there is a better solution

Obama Is Not Embracing Eradication

The [Barack] Obama administration believes previous counter-narcotics efforts that focused on destroying crops drove many farmers and influential tribesmen into supporting the Islamist insurgency. So the U.S. and British governments have taken a hands-off approach to an eradication program in which Afghan soldiers burn or plow under fields of poppy before the crop can be harvested. Instead, special forces troops . . . are active in finding and interdicting the routes used to smuggle poppy resin from Afghanistan to processing plants thought to be in Iran and Pakistan.

The Afghan government also is trying to persuade farmers to stop growing poppy and shift to other crops, particularly wheat. The U.S. and British governments are underwriting a program to give farmers high-grade wheat seed and fertilizer at a reduced price. . . .

Tony Perry,
"Marines Plow Ahead with Anti-Poppy
Campaign In Afghan District," Los Angeles Times,
November 29, 2009. www.latimes.com.

for stabilizing the country than adding 17,000 American soldiers to the 38,000 already there. Without an effective strategy to turn the situation around, the surge is likely to result in the unnecessary loss of human lives and billions of dollars, while failing to remove the major reason for the instability in the region—the heroin trade.

There is, however, a strategy that could reduce the cost of fighting terrorists and drug traffickers alike, while helping to establish a self-sustaining economy in Afghanistan and defusing the tensions in the region. It would also cut down on the social and economic cost of heroin use in the U.S.

The Obama administration should implement an innovative and safe poppy eradication method that previous U.S. governments spent billions of dollars developing. Mycoherbicides are naturally occurring fungi that are used to control such illicit pest plants as the opium poppy and other noxious weeds. Unlike chemical controls now in use, mycoherbicides assail only the targeted plant, rendering its cultivation uneconomical. These fungi continue to live in the soil, preventing the future growth of the opium poppy plant, but are harmless to other crops, to humans and to the environment.

On Dec. 29, 2006, then president George W. Bush signed Public Law 109/469, of which Section 1111 requires the Office of National Drug Control Policy to conduct an efficacy study of mycoherbicides' use on the opium poppy and coca shrub. Yet the one-year study was never conducted, apparently because the drug czar's office prefers to use pesticides for eradication. Concluding these studies should become a priority for the Obama administration.

The use of mycoherbicides in Afghanistan, combined with adequate enforcement by the military, will mitigate the production of heroin and cut off the terrorists' major money supply. This would free up the $150 to $200 billion now used to fight the drug trade and its by-products—crime, addiction, diseases, accidents, etc.—in the U.S., and make these funds available to help fight terrorism directly.

Implementing this new strategy, while subsidizing the Afghan economy until other crops and industries can replace the illegal heroin trade, which leaves most Afghans poor, seems a better way for America to succeed in fighting terrorism and endemic corruption. It would also free up resources for an array of social and governmental reforms, which should be clearly defined and strictly supervised. With no heroin to fund terrorism and subvert the economies and political systems of Afghanistan and Pakistan, the American agenda could take a huge leap forward.

| "Persistent eradication over several years has worked well in Latin America, and it may also be an important part of the solution in Afghanistan, but not in the absence of alternative livelihoods and interdiction."

The United States Should Concentrate on Interdiction of the Drug Trade in Afghanistan

Beth DeGrasse and Ylli Bajraktari

Beth DeGrasse and Ylli Bajraktari work in the Center for Post-Conflict Peace and Stability Operations at the United States Institute of Peace. In the following viewpoint, the authors argue that the drug trade is central to the economy of Afghanistan and that it helps fund terror and corruption. However, they argue that eradication of crops alone generally hurts farmers, not traffickers who simply raise the price of their stock. Therefore, DeGrasse and Bajraktari say, a solution will require interdiction and an effort to move farmers to new crops. They conclude that solving the problem may take more than a decade.

Beth DeGrasse and Ylli Bajraktari, "Dealing with the Illicit Drug Trade: The Afghan Quandary," USIP.org, April, 2005. Reproduced by permission.

As you read, consider the following questions:

1. According to the authors, why would eliminating the drug trade make stable government in Afghanistan impossible?

2. How much did CENTCOM's counter-narcotics budget increase between 2002 and 2004?

3. What three conditions must exist if eradication is to be effective, according to the authors?

One of the greatest challenges to post-conflict Afghanistan is the alarming increase in poppy cultivation. Since the ousting of the Taliban regime, large-scale opium production and trafficking has hindered legitimate economic development and stable governance, shifting the focus of the international community from stabilization and reconstruction to combating narcotics.

Afghanistan Depends on the Drug Trade

One of the poorest nations on earth, Afghanistan faces a dilemma. Efforts to establish a stable government based on the rule of law are severely undermined by the fact that nearly 40 percent of the nation's economy is dependent upon an illegal drug trade. But if Afghanistan were to eliminate the source of 40 percent of its revenue without providing a substitute, achieving a stable government based on the rule of law would be impossible.

The U.S. Institute of Peace brought together 50 experts, drawn from the U.S. government, the Afghanistan government, academia, think tanks, and international and nongovernmental organizations to discuss narcotics trafficking in Afghanistan, including issues of eradication, interdiction and crop substitution at an off-the-record session of its Afghanistan Working Group. . . .

Participants in the session pointed out that as narcotics production in Latin America declines, Afghanistan has become a major hub for cultivation of poppy and production of opium. According to international narcotics experts, 61,000 hectares of poppy fields covering an estimated 20 percent of the arable land in Afghanistan are under cultivation today [2005] as compared to under 30,000 hectares in 1994 and around 2,000 hectares in 2001. Poppy cultivation in Afghanistan today generates an estimated $2.8 billion in total annual revenue, according to working group participants.

The dramatic increase in the narcotics trade has broad implications for Afghanistan's political, economic and social development, participants said. Control over narcotics activity by powerful warlords, some of whom hold positions in the government of Afghan President Hamid Karzai, undermines the authority of the central government. Cultivation and export revenue lines the pockets of Taliban [a radical Islamist group; they lead the insurgency in Afghanistan] diehards, [terrorist group] al Qaeda members, and others opposed to democracy in Afghanistan, according to some working group members. Drug money is recycled into legitimate enterprises, making the entire economy dependent on poppy cultivation.

Narcotics Fund Terror

The United States intervened in Afghanistan in 2001 to remove the Taliban regime [in power from 1996] that supported and allowed al Qaeda camps to flourish in its territory. The U.S. military remains in Afghanistan both to capture the remaining al Qaeda leaders and to create conditions that will prevent terrorists from returning. Working group participants noted that this cannot be done without combating illicit narcotics, which provide funding not only for corrupt officials, warlords, and traffickers, but also for the remaining Taliban and al Qaeda cadres.

Learning from Drug Policies in Latin America

The [Barack] Obama administration could learn valuable lessons from some of its Latin American counterparts. First, it could recognize that the international drug control policies implemented over the past several decades have failed to make any significant dent in the supply of illicit drugs. Second, it could adopt measures that reduce the harm caused by both drug use and the "war on drugs." Completely eliminating the demand or production of illicit drugs is simply not achievable. The challenge, therefore, is to put into place policies that mitigate the harm caused by drug use to individuals, families, and communities, and the harm or negative consequences caused by illicit drug production and the policies intended to contain it. . . .

One very significant and immediate step that the Obama administration should take is to end support for fumigation and other forced eradication efforts. Then, it should redirect funding for those ineffective, cruel, and flawed approaches to development programs that support alternative livelihoods. Forced eradication efforts have generated some of the most extensive collateral damage from the U.S. "war on drugs"—without making a significant impact toward reducing the production of coca or poppies (the raw material for heroin). Ending this war on poor farmers is a fundamental step toward developing international drug control policies that are both more effective and more humane.

Coletta Youngers, "Beyond the Drug War,"
Foreign Policy in Focus, *November 25, 2008. www.fpif.org.*

Given this, the strategy of the United States and its coalition partners is to build a strong state that can uphold the rule of law, according to several people at the meeting. The U.S. Central Command (CENTCOM) [a U.S. armed forces command unit responsible for Middle East deployments] budget for counter-narcotics efforts grew from just $1 million in 2002 to $73 million last year [2004], but the focus of U.S. counter-narcotics efforts in Afghanistan remains assistance to the government in [capital city] Kabul, including funds for:

- *Capacity Building.* The Departments of Defense and State and the U.S. Drug Enforcement Administration are providing training and equipment for new counter-narcotics special units, specializing in eradication and interdiction.

- *Logistics Assistance.* The Department of Defense is helping to establish a base outside of Kabul for counter-narcotics efforts, creating intelligence databases and providing counter-narcotics units with air transportation.

- *Coordination.* The United States is also helping to facilitate intelligence sharing; information sharing among border police, highway police and national police; and coordination among border police of neighboring states. Participants at the meeting generally agreed that it would be a mistake for the U.S. military to get directly involved in pursuing drug traffickers in Afghanistan. Nonetheless, some suggested that when cooperating with warlords in the pursuit of al Qaeda, the U.S. military should make it clear that drug trafficking is unacceptable.

Eradication Does Not Hurt Traffickers

Poor Afghan farmers grow poppy in order to pay debts, participants noted. Their payments are normally made in fixed quantities of opium that are determined well in advance of the harvest. If they fall short in their payments, the farmers become increasingly indebted to drug traffickers and have to produce even more opium at the next harvest or face dire consequences. This vicious cycle can be broken by providing farmers with legitimate alternative livelihoods, which enable them to survive without poppy cultivation, and by interdicting the drug trade, which lowers the demand for poppy and reduces prices.

There is evidence that persistent eradication over several years has worked well in Latin America, and it may also be an important part of the solution in Afghanistan, but not in the absence of alternative livelihoods and interdiction. Without alternatives and interdiction, eradication causes farmers to fall short in paying their debts, raises the farm-gate price [the price of a crop sold directly from the farm] and encourages more planting of poppy. Traffickers, who maintain substantial stocks of opium, can benefit from higher prices (by selling their stocks), but farmers, who generally have no stocks, cannot. Eradication can be effective in a particular area if farmers have viable and profitable alternatives, if interdiction has destroyed drug traffickers' stocks, and if there is a general expectation that the rule of law will prevail. Therefore, the participants contended, there is a need for a balanced approach, with eradication, interdiction and state-building all essential components.

Getting the policy mix right will not be easy, and even then it will take a long time to displace opium from its predominant role in the economy of Afghanistan. A decade or more of sustained effort will be required to break the economic links among drug traffickers, terrorists, warlords and corrupt officials, the working group concluded.

"*The illegal drug industry is driven by demand: As long as some people want drugs, other people will find ways to supply them.*"

Neither Eradication nor Interdiction Will Stop the Drug Trade in Afghanistan

Eugene Robinson

Eugene Robinson is an associate editor and columnist at the Washington Post. *In the following viewpoint, he argues, based on his experience in Latin America, that there is no way to stop illegal drug production. He notes that eradication would turn farmers against the United States, while targeting middlemen would be difficult in a country with a weak government where officials are vulnerable to bribery. Robinson concludes that the U.S. effort to defeat the drug trade in Afghanistan is doomed.*

As you read, consider the following questions:

1. According to Robinson, who introduced the poppy to Afghanistan?

2. Who is Ahmed Wali Karzai, and what does the author assert is his alleged involvement in the drug trade?

Eugene Robinson, "A Familiar War in Afghanistan," *The Washington Post*, October 30, 2009. Copyright © 2009, *The Washington Post*. Reprinted with permission.

3. How does Robinson translate *plata o plomo*, offered to Latin American officials?

The opium poppy was introduced to Afghanistan more than 2,300 years ago by the armies of Alexander the Great. His forces were eventually driven out, like those of every would-be conqueror since. The poppy has proved more tenacious.

On Monday, three U.S. Drug Enforcement Administration [DEA] agents—Forrest Leamon, Chad Michael and Michael Weston, all from the Washington area—were killed in a helicopter crash in western Afghanistan. U.S. officials have released few details about the incident. The *Times* of London reported that the aircraft was shot down after a raid on the compound of a prominent Afghan drug lord.

On Wednesday, the *New York Times* reported that the CIA has been making regular payments to a suspected major figure in the Afghan opium trade: Ahmed Wali Karzai, the brother of President Hamid Karzai. The newspaper quoted sources alleging that Ahmed Wali Karzai—who denies any involvement in the drug business—collects "huge" fees from traffickers for allowing trucks loaded with drugs to cross bridges he controls in the southern part of the country.

So is it our policy to attack the Afghan drug trade while we also line the pockets of one of its reputed kingpins? Who is going to explain this to the families of agents Leamon, Michael and Weston?

Afghanistan's status as a narco-superpower is another reason why President [Barack] Obama would be wrong to deepen U.S. involvement. Opium is the one booming sector of the Afghan economy: Poppy fields in the south and west of the country produce the raw material for an estimated 90 percent of the world's heroin. Money from the opium trade supports the resurgent Taliban, which is fighting to expel U.S. and NATO forces. Therefore, a blow against the drug business is a blow against the enemy.

Except when it isn't. Except when the "good guys" who are supposed to be our allies—and many of the Afghan citizens whom a counterinsurgency strategy would try to protect—are dependent on the drug trade as well. Except when the corruption that is an intrinsic element of the drug business not only blurs the line between friend and foe but also obscures the difference between right and wrong in a thick fog of moral ambiguity.

As the *Post*'s South America correspondent during the administration of George Bush the Elder, I watched firsthand our government's costly and futile crusade against the cocaine industry. We tried attacking the problem in the coca fields—I visited a U.S.-financed military base in Peru's Upper Huallaga Valley, where at the time 60 percent of the world's coca was grown. We tried going after the processors—in Colombia, police took me to a jungle camp where chemists had been hard at work just hours earlier. We tried breaking up the trafficking cartels—I was served lunch at a Medellin prison by three cocaine bosses whose comfortable incarceration was almost like an extended stay at a hotel.

Nothing worked. All the United States managed to do was shift the coca fields from one valley to the next and break the big cartels into smaller ones. Profits from the drug trade still sustain a guerrilla insurgency in Colombia that has controlled huge swaths of the countryside for more than four decades. Meanwhile, cocaine is readily available throughout the United States. The illegal drug industry is driven by demand: As long as some people want drugs, other people will find ways to supply them.

DEA officials have said they are sharply increasing the agency's presence in Afghanistan. Wisely, the Obama administration is abandoning the George W. Bush–era strategy of trying to eradicate the poppy fields; eradication, which robs rural communities of their only livelihood, may be the quickest and surest way to turn apolitical farmers into anti-American insur-

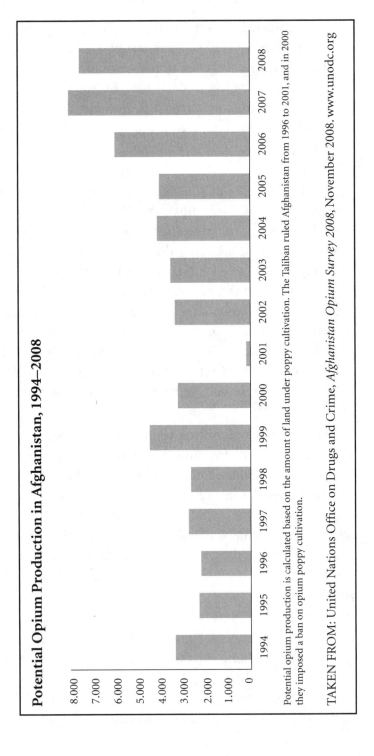

Potential Opium Production in Afghanistan, 1994–2008

Potential opium production is calculated based on the amount of land under poppy cultivation. The Taliban ruled Afghanistan from 1996 to 2001, and in 2000 they imposed a ban on opium poppy cultivation.

TAKEN FROM: United Nations Office on Drugs and Crime, *Afghanistan Opium Survey 2008*, November 2008. www.unodc.org

gents. The focus now is on the middlemen who buy, transport and process the drugs—which creates a different kind of problem.

Those middlemen logically seek, and obtain, official protection. In Latin America, they approach police and government officials with an offer of *plata o plomo*—silver or lead—meaning the officials can choose to accept the bribes they are being offered, or they can choose to be shot. In a country as poor as Afghanistan, with such weak central authority, the U.S.-backed government is vulnerable to bribery at almost every level.

The inevitable future is one in which we attack and support the Afghan drug trade at the same time. Is this a policy for which we can ask DEA agents to give their lives?

| "Licensing and regulating poppy cultiva-
tion would not only create stability and
economic development, it could sap
support for the Taliban and help win
the war in Afghanistan."

Poppies Should Be Legalized in Afghanistan

Reza Aslan

*Reza Aslan is a fellow at the University of Southern California's
Center on Public Diplomacy and a Middle East analyst for CBS
News. In the following viewpoint, he argues that efforts to eliminate the drug trade in Afghanistan have failed. He suggests,
therefore, that instead of fighting poppy production, the Afghan
government should license growers to produce poppies for medical use and tax the resulting crops. He argues that this would
create stability and economic development in Afghanistan and
would reduce support for the Taliban, helping the United States
win the Afghan war.*

As you read, consider the following questions:

1. To what does Aslan attribute the reduction in poppy
   production between 2007 and 2008?

Reza Aslan, "How Opium Can Save Afghanistan," *The Daily Beast*, December 19, 2008.

2. Where does the author assert poppy for medicine programs have proved successful?

3. According to Aslan, how much of the world's population faces a shortage of morphine?

Afghanistan may be one [of] the poorest countries in the world, but by legalizing and licensing opium production it could conceivably become the Saudi Arabia of morphine.

No Progress on Eradication

It is a measure of just how great a failure the counter-narcotics strategy in Afghanistan has been that, after six consecutive years of record growth [as of 2008] in poppy production, including a staggering 20 percent increase last year alone, American and UN [United Nations] officials are actually patting themselves on the back over a 6 percent decline in 2008. "We are finally seeing the results of years of effort," said Antonio Maria Costa, who heads the United Nations Office on Drugs and Crime.

Yet this meager decline has almost nothing to do with international eradication efforts and everything to do with the law of supply and demand. As the *New York Times* reported in November, the Taliban [extreme Islamists leading the Afghan insurgency] have begun forcibly curbing poppy production and stockpiling opium in order to boost prices, which had fallen sharply due to a glut in the market. Indeed, Afghanistan has produced so much opium—between 90 to 95 percent of the world's supply—that prices have dropped nearly 20 percent.

The truth is that the poppy eradication effort in Afghanistan, which consists mostly of hacking away at poppy fields with sticks and sickles, or spraying them from above with deadly herbicides, has been nothing short of a disaster. All this policy has managed to achieve (excluding that vaunted 6 percent decrease) is to alienate the Afghan people, fuel support for the Taliban, and further weaken the government of President Hamid Karzai, whose own brother has been linked to the illegal opium trade. Meanwhile, poppy cultivation is now such an entrenched part of Afghanistan's economy that in some parts of the country, opium is considered legal tender, replacing cash in day-to-day transactions.

In spite of all this, the U.S. State Department is planning to expand its crop eradication campaign. In 2007, President [George W.] Bush tapped the former ambassador to Colombia, William Wood, to become U.S. Ambassador to Afghanistan. Wood, whose nickname in Colombia was "Chemical Bill," because of his enthusiasm for aerial fumigation, has been charged with implementing in Afghanistan the same crop eradication program that—despite five billion dollars and hundreds of tons of chemicals—has had little effect on Colombia's coca production.

The Sole Successful Export

It is time to admit that the struggle to end poppy cultivation in Afghanistan is a losing battle. The fact is that opium has long been Afghanistan's sole successful export. Poppy seeds cost little to buy, can grow pretty much anywhere, and offer a huge return on a farmer's investment. Only the Taliban has ever managed to significantly reduce opium production in the country (as it did during its late-1990s rule)—a feat managed by executing anyone caught growing poppies. It is no exaggeration to say that we have a better chance of defeating the Taliban than putting a dent in Afghanistan's opium trade. So then, as the saying goes: If you can't beat them, join them.

The International Council on Security and Development (ICOS), a policy think tank with offices in London and [Afghan capital] Kabul, has proposed abandoning the futile eradication efforts in Afghanistan and instead licensing farmers to legally grow poppies for the production of medical morphine. This so-called "Poppy for Medicine" program is not as crazy

Global Morphine Needs, 2005

Region	Disease	Number of deaths in 2005	Estimated number of patients in moderate to severe pain	Morphine treatment period (days)	Daily dosage (milligrams)	Estimated need (metric tons)	Actual use (metric tons)	Unmet need (metric tons)
Eastern Europe & Central Asia	HIV/AIDS	53,000	26,500	600	120	1.9	0.598	8.9
	Cancer	780,000	351,000	180	120	7.6		
Asia	HIV/AIDS	633,000	317,000	600	120	22.8	0.637	57.0
	Cancer	3,580,000	1,610,000	180	120	34.8		
Sub-Saharan Africa	HIV/AIDS	2,000,000	1,000,000	600	120	72.0	0.228	76.5
	Cancer	460,000	207,000	180	120	4.5		
Latin America	HIV/AIDS	59,000	29,500	600	120	2.1	0.577	6.6
	Cancer	519,000	234,000	180	120	5.0		
Global	HIV/AIDS	2,800,000	1,400,000	600	120	100.8	31.8	142.9
	Cancer	7,600,000	3,420,000	180	120	73.9		

TAKEN FROM: "Global Need for Morphine," *Poppy for Medicine.* www.poppyformedicine.net.

as it may sound. Similar programs have already proven successful in Turkey and India, both of which were able to bring the illegal production of opium in their countries under control by licensing, regulating, and taxing poppy cultivation. And there is every reason to believe that the program could work even in a fractured country like Afghanistan. This is because the entire production process—from poppies to pills— would occur inside the village under strict control of village authorities, which, in Afghanistan, often trump the authority of the federal government. Licensed farmers would legally plant and cultivate poppy seeds. Factories built in the villages would transform the poppies into morphine tablets. The tablets would then be shipped off to Kabul, where they would be exported to the rest of the world. These rural village communities would experience significant economic development, and tax revenues would stream into Kabul. (The Taliban, which tax poppy cultivation under their control at 10 percent, made $300 million dollars in 2007.)

The global demand for poppy-based medicine is as great as it is for oil. According to the International Narcotics Control Board, 80 percent of the world's population currently faces a shortage of morphine; morphine prices have skyrocketed as a result. The ICOS estimates that Afghanistan could supply this market with all the morphine it needs, and at a price at least 55 percent lower than the current market average.

The War on Drugs and the War on Terror

The Bush administration balked at this idea, despite a warm reception from the Afghan government and some NATO allies. There has been a fear in Washington [DC] that such a proposal would contradict America's avowed "war on drugs." But the opium crisis in Afghanistan is not a drug enforcement problem, it is a national security issue: Licensing and regulating poppy cultivation would not only create stability and economic development, it could sap support for the Taliban and help win the war in Afghanistan.

So which will it be? The war on drugs? Or the war on terror? When it comes to Afghanistan, we can only choose one.

Periodical Bibliography

The following articles have been selected to supplement the diverse views presented in this chapter.

Associated Press	"U.S. to Shift Approach to Afghanistan Drug Trade," *Los Angeles Times*, June 28, 2009.
Associated Press	"Without Opium, Afghan Village Economy Spirals," MSNBC.com, August 2, 2009. www.msnbc.com.
Scott Baldauf	"Afghanistan Riddled with Drug Ties," *Christian Science Monitor*, May 13, 2005.
Michel Chossudovsky	"Who Benefits from the Afghan Opium Trade?" GlobalResearch.ca, September 21, 2006. www.globalresearch.ca.
Vanda Felbab-Brown	"Target the Drug Lords in Afghanistan, Not the Farmers," Brookings Institution, July 15, 2009. www.brookings.edu.
Dexter Filkins	"Poppies a Target in Fight Against Taliban," *New York Times*, April 28, 2009.
Jonathan Owen	"As Deaths in Afghanistan Rise, So Does Growth of Opium," *Independent*, November 22, 2009. www.independent.co.uk.
Matthew Rosenberg	"U.N. Reports a Decline in Afghanistan's Opium Trade," *Wall Street Journal*, September 2, 2009.
Thomas Schweich	"Is Afghanistan a Narco-State?" *New York Times*, July 27, 2009.
Vivienne Walt	"Report: Afghanistan's Opium Boom May Be Over," *Time*, September 2, 2009. www.time.com.

For Further Discussion

Chapter 1

1. Jeremy Shapiro, in his interview with Gregor Peter Schmitz, and H.D.S. Greenway both suggest that more American troops would not be helpful in Afghanistan. What reasons do they give, and how do these reasons differ?

2. What reasons does David H. Petraeus give for continuing U.S. involvement in Afghanistan? Would Richard N. Haass find these reasons convincing?

Chapter 2

1. Eliza Szabo says U.S. forces are "unable or unwilling" to adopt tactics that would decrease civilian death tolls in Afghanistan. According to David Zucchino, is the problem for U.S. forces a lack of ability to reduce civilian deaths or a lack of willingness? What evidence does he provide to support this position?

2. Based on the viewpoints by Ellen Goodman and Anand Gopal, has the United States managed to significantly improve the status of Afghan women? In your view, what steps could the United States take to improve women's positions in Afghan society?

Chapter 3

1. Jake Tapper and Sunlen Miller report in their viewpoint that the White House called Hamid Karzai's election "legitimate," but not "credible." What is the difference between "legitimate" and "credible"? After reading the viewpoint by Peter W. Galbraith, would you agree that Karzai has passed the test of legitimacy, if not of credibility? Explain your reasoning.

2. What evidence does Christian Brose provide that Afghans are ready for democracy? What evidence do Thomas H. Johnson and M. Chris Mason provide that Afghanistan is not prepared for democracy? Which viewpoint do you believe makes the more convincing argument?

Chapter 4

1. Julien Mercille argues that the main beneficiaries of drug money are warlords allied with the Afghan government, not Taliban rebels. If Mercille is correct, would this undermine Rachel Ehrenfeld's arguments? Explain how and why.

2. Reza Aslan argues that legalizing poppy cultivation would solve many of Afghanistan's problems. Based on the viewpoint by Beth DeGrasse and Ylli Bajraktari, what problems would remain for Afghanistan? For example, what hurdles might the Afghan government face in imposing the taxes that Aslan proposes?

Organizations to Contact

The editors have compiled the following list of organizations concerned with the issues debated in this book. The descriptions are derived from materials provided by the organizations. All have publications or information available for interested readers. The list was compiled on the date of publication of the present volume; the information provided here may change. Be aware that many organizations take several weeks or longer to respond to inquiries, so allow as much time as possible.

Afghan Red Crescent Society
PO Box 3066, Kabul
  Afghanistan
0093 752 014446 • fax: 0093 752 023476
e-mail: int.relation.arcs.@gmail.com
Web site: www.ifrc.org/address/af.asp

The Afghan Red Crescent Society is an affiliate of the International Federation of Red Cross and Red Crescent Societies, the world's largest humanitarian organization, which provides relief assistance around the world. The Red Crescent is used in place of the Red Cross in many Islamic countries. The group's mission is to improve the lives of vulnerable people, especially those who are victims of natural disasters, poverty, wars, and health emergencies. The Web site includes a section on "Where We Work," which provides specific information about the group's activities in Afghanistan.

Afghanistan Relief Organization (ARO)
PO Box 866, Cypress, CA   90630
(877) 276-2440 • fax: (714) 661-5932
Web site: www.afghanrelief.org

The Afghanistan Relief Organization (ARO) is a humanitarian organization established in 1998 in response to the economic and physical hardships suffered by the Afghan people after decades of war. A volunteer organization funded by public donations, ARO provides relief supplies and runs a number of health, literacy, and other programs to help the poor in Afghanistan. The ARO Web site contains an overview of Afghanistan, materials teachers can use to educate students about Afghanistan, and links to newsletters discussing ARO news and activities.

Human Rights Watch (HRW)

350 Fifth Avenue, 34th Floor, New York, NY 10118-3299
(212) 290-4700
e-mail: hrwnyc@hrw.org
Web site: www.hrw.org

Human Rights Watch (HRW) is an independent organization dedicated to defending and protecting human rights around the world. It seeks to focus international attention on places where human rights are violated, to give voices to the oppressed, and to hold oppressors accountable for their crimes. The HRW Web site includes numerous reports on human rights in Afghanistan, including *Afghanistan: Return of the Warlords* and *Afghanistan: US Investigation of Airstrike Deaths 'Deeply Flawed'*.

Institute for Afghan Studies (IAS)

e-mail: info@institute-for-afghan-studies.org
Web site: www.institute-for-afghan-studies.org

Funded and managed by young Afghan scholars from around the world, the Institute for Afghan Studies (IAS) seeks to promote a better understanding of Afghanistan through scholarly research and studies. The IAS Web site provides a wealth of information on the history and politics of Afghanistan, including weekly political analyses, reports and articles, and biographical information on key figures in Afghanistan's politics. Examples of publications include *One Scary Voter Registration at a Time* and *Afghan Economy in the War and Pre-War Period*.

Islamic Republic of Afghanistan/Office of the President
Web site: www.president.gov.af

The central Web site of the Afghanistan government provides information on Afghanistan's president, national assembly, constitution, cabinet, departments, and commissions. It contains news reports, presidential speeches and decrees, press releases and statements, and links to other government-affiliated Web sites.

NATO in Afghanistan
Web site: www.nato.int/issues/afghanistan/index.html

NATO in Afghanistan is part of the official Web site of the North Atlantic Treaty Organization (NATO), an alliance of twenty-six countries from Europe and North America committed to fulfilling the joint security goals of the 1949 North Atlantic Treaty. The Afghanistan section of the Web site provides an overview of NATO's interests and mission in Afghanistan and includes a link to the International Security Assistance Force (ISAF), a NATO military initiative that provides support to the Afghan government to help with security, reconstruction, and development. The Web site includes news articles, press releases, speeches, and transcripts relating to NATO's role in Afghanistan.

Revolutionary Association of the Women of Afghanistan (RAWA)
PO Box 374, Quetta
  Pakistan
0092 300 5541258
Web site: www.rawa.org

The Revolutionary Association of the Women of Afghanistan (RAWA) was established in Kabul, Afghanistan, in 1977 as an independent political/social organization of Afghan women fighting for peace, freedom, and democracy in Afghanistan. The founders were a number of female Afghan intellectuals whose objective was to involve all Afghan women in acquiring human rights and establishing an Afghan government based on democratic and secular values. RAWA also solicits public donations for relief aid and projects to assist schools, orphanages, and women's cooperatives. RAWA's Web site includes press statements and speeches as well as links to news, reports, and articles on political, social, and economic issues in Afghanistan.

United Nations Development Programme (UNDP)
1 United Nations Plaza, New York, NY   10017
(212) 906-5000 • fax: (212) 906-5001
Web site: www.undp.org

The United Nations Development Programme (UNDP) is an organization created by the United Nations to promote global development and to help connect developing countries with knowledge, experience, and resources to help their people build a better life. Among other activities, the UNDP coordinates the efforts to reach the Millennium Development Goals, a commitment by world leaders to cut world poverty in half by 2015. The Web site includes a number of relevant publications, including *Fast Facts: UNDP in Afghanistan* and *Afghanistan: Disbandment of Illegal Armed Groups*.

U.S.-Afghan Women's Council
PO Box 571485, Washington, DC   20057
(202) 687-5095 • fax: (202) 687-1954
e-mail: ew245@georgetown.edu
Web site: http://gucchd.georgetown.edu/76315.html

The U.S.-Afghan Women's Council, a project of the U.S. State Department, was created to promote private/public partnerships between U.S. and Afghan institutions and mobilize private resources to help Afghan women gain skills and education to play a role in the reconstruction of Afghanistan. The council is now associated with Georgetown University. The Web site includes the council's newsletter, *Connections*, as well as news, speeches, fact sheets, press releases, and information on projects affecting Afghan women.

U.S. Department of State

2201 C Street NW, Washington, DC   20520
(202) 647-4000
Web site: www.state.gov

The U.S. Department of State is a federal agency that advises the president on issues of foreign policy. Its Web site includes the section "Countries," which provides a great deal of information about the country of Afghanistan, including an overview of the nation and materials relating to reconstruction, U.S. aid, and NATO's involvement in the country. Publications available through the Web site include *U.S. Forces in Afghanistan* and *NATO in Afghanistan: A Test of the Transatlantic Alliance.*

Bibliography of Books

Cheryl Benard
and Nina
Hachigian, eds.

Democracy and Islam in the New Constitution of Afghanistan. Santa Monica, CA: RAND Corporation, 2003.

Sarah Chayes

The Punishment of Virtue: Inside Afghanistan After the Taliban. New York: Penguin Press, 2006.

Steve Coll

Ghost Wars: The Secret History of the CIA, Afghanistan, and Bin Laden, from the Soviet Invasion to September 10, 2001. New York: Penguin Books, 2004.

Robert D. Crews
and Amin Tarzi,
eds.

The Taliban and the Crisis of Afghanistan. Cambridge, MA: Harvard University Press, 2008.

Gregory Feifer

The Great Gamble: The Soviet War in Afghanistan. New York: HarperCollins, 2009.

Paul Fitzgerald
and Elizabeth
Gould

Invisible History: Afghanistan's Untold Story. San Francisco, CA: City Lights Books, 2009.

Antonio Giustozzi

Koran, Kalashnikov, and Laptop: The Neo-Taliban Insurgency in Afghanistan. New York: Columbia University Press, 2008.

Joel Hafvenstein

Opium Season: A Year on the Afghan Frontier. Guilford, CT: Lyons Press, 2007.

Seth G. Jones   *In the Graveyard of Empires: America's War in Afghanistan.* New York: W.W. Norton & Company, 2009.

Sonali Kolhatkar   *Bleeding Afghanistan: Washington,* and James Ingalls   *Warlords, and the Propaganda of Silence.* New York: Seven Stories Press, 2006.

Eric V. Larson   *Misfortunes of War: Press and Public* and Bogdan   *Reactions to Civilian Deaths in* Savych   *Wartime.* Santa Monica, CA: RAND Corporation, 2007.

David Loyn   *In Afghanistan: Two Hundred Years of British, Russian and American Occupation.* New York: Palgrave Macmillan, 2009.

David MacDonald *Drugs in Afghanistan: Opium, Outlaws and Scorpion Tales.* London: Pluto Press, 2007.

David R. Mares   *Drug Wars and Coffeehouses: The Political Economy of the International Drug Trade.* Washington, DC: CQ Press, 2006.

Nick B. Mills   *Karzai: The Failing American Intervention and the Struggle for Afghanistan.* Hoboken, NJ: John Wiley & Sons, 2007.

Matthew J.   *A Democracy Is Born: An Insider's* Morgan   *Account of the Battle Against Terrorism in Afghanistan.* Westport, CT: Praeger Security International, 2007.

Leigh Neville	*Special Operations Forces in Afghanistan: Afghanistan 2001–2007.* Oxford, UK: Osprey Publishing, 2008.
Gretchen Peters	*Seeds of Terror: How Heroin Is Bankrolling the Taliban and al Qaeda.* New York: St. Martin's Press, 2009.
Ahmed Rashid	*Descent into Chaos: The U.S. and the Disaster in Pakistan, Afghanistan, and Central Asia.* New York: Penguin Books, 2009.
Ahmed Rashid	*Taliban: Islam, Oil and the New Great Game in Central Asia.* New York: I.B. Tauris & Co., 2008.
Robert I. Rotberg, ed.	*Corruption, Global Security, and World Order.* Cambridge, MA: World Peace Foundation, 2009.
Barnett R. Rubin	*Afghanistan's Uncertain Transition from Turmoil to Normalcy.* New York: Council on Foreign Relations, 2006.
"Sulima" and "Hala" as told to Batya Swift Yasgur	*Behind the Burqa: Our Life in Afghanistan and How We Escaped to Freedom.* Hoboken, NJ: John Wiley & Sons, 2002.
Stephen Tanner	*Afghanistan: A Military History from Alexander the Great to the War Against the Taliban.* Philadelphia, PA: Da Capo Press, 2009.

Mariam Abou Zahab and Oliver Roy   *Islamist Networks: The Afghan-Pakistan Connection.* Translated by John King. New York: Columbia University Press, 2004.

Index